EYE ON
ART

Leonardo da Vinci
Renaissance Genius

By Tamra B. Orr

Portions of this book originally appeared in *Leonardo da Vinci* by Don Nardo.

LUCENT
P R E S S

Published in 2019 by
Lucent Press, an Imprint of Greenhaven Publishing, LLC
353 3rd Avenue
Suite 255
New York, NY 10010

Designer: Deanna Paternostro
Editor: Melissa Raé Shofner

Library of Congress Cataloging-in-Publication Data

Names: Orr, Tamra, author.
Title: Leonardo da Vinci : Renaissance genius / Tamra B. Orr.
Description: New York : Lucent Press, 2019. | Series: Eye on art | Includes
  bibliographical references and index.
Identifiers: LCCN 2018022795 (print) | LCCN 2018025752 (ebook) | ISBN
  9781534565333 (eBook) | ISBN 9781534565326 (library bound book) | ISBN
  9781534565319 (pbk. book)
Subjects: LCSH: Leonardo, da Vinci, 1452-1519–Juvenile literature. |
  Artists–Italy–Biography–Juvenile literature. | Art,
  Renaissance–Italy–Juvenile literature.
Classification: LCC N6923.L33 (ebook) | LCC N6923.L33 O77 2019 (print) | DDC
  709.2 [B] –dc23
LC record available at https://lccn.loc.gov/2018022795

Printed in the United States of America

CPSIA compliance information: Batch #BW19KL: For further information contact Greenhaven Publishing LLC, New York, New York at 1-844-317-7404.

Please visit our website, www.greenhavenpublishing.com. For a free color catalog of all our high-quality
books, call toll free 1-844-317-7404 or fax 1-844-317-7405.

Contents

Foreword

What is art? There is no one answer to that question. Every person has a different idea of what makes something a work of art. Some people think of art as the work of masters such as Leonardo da Vinci, Mary Cassatt, or Michelangelo. Others see artistic beauty in everything from skyscrapers and animated films to fashion shows and graffiti. Everyone brings their own point of view to their interpretation of art.

Discovering the hard work and pure talent behind artistic techniques from different periods in history and different places around the world helps people develop an appreciation for art in all its varied forms. The stories behind great works of art and the artists who created them have fascinated people for many years and continue to do so today. Whether a person has a passion for painting, graphic design, or another creative pursuit, learning about the lives of great artists and the paths that can be taken to achieve success as an artist in the modern world can inspire budding creators to pursue their dreams.

This series introduces readers to different artistic styles, as well as the artists who made those styles famous. As they read about creative expression in the past and present, they are challenged to think critically about their own definition of art.

Quotes from artists, art historians, and other experts provide a unique perspective on each topic, and a detailed bibliography is provided as a starting place for further research. In addition, a list of websites and books about each topic encourages readers to continue their exploration of the fascinating world of art.

This world comes alive with each turn of the page, as readers explore sidebars about the artistic process and creative careers. Essential examples of different artistic styles are presented in the form of vibrant photographs and historical images, giving readers a comprehensive look at art history from ancient times to the present.

Art may be difficult to define, but it is easy to appreciate. In developing a deeper understanding of different art forms, readers will be able to look at the world around them with a fresh perspective on the beauty that can be found in unexpected places.

A True Polymath

Not many people encounter the word "polymath" very often, if at all. As rare as the word is, so is the subject of its definition. A polymath is a person who solves problems by using complex areas of knowledge. Polymaths are known for having such wide-ranging bases of knowledge that they can come up with ideas, concepts, and solutions that the average person would never think of. No person throughout history personifies the polymath more than Leonardo da Vinci. Despite the fact that he was born in a small city in Italy, had no formal education, and lived in difficult, war-torn times, he was what many refer to today as a universal genius or Renaissance man.

Leonardo was a man of almost unlimited talents—he was an artist, inventor, and scholar. Born in the mid-1400s, he was part of the Renaissance, which was a period of great cultural and artistic achievement that began in Italy in the mid-1300s and later spread across most of the rest of Europe. During the Renaissance, everyone from European writers, painters, and sculptors to architects and city planners produced an explosion of brilliant achievements.

Amid this immense cultural output, a number of individuals distinguished themselves by excelling at or mastering several areas of knowledge and expertise. By the 19th century, this type of multitalented person was referred to as a Renaissance man or Renaissance woman. At the time, however, the term most commonly used was universal man or woman. One of Leonardo's highest goals was the constant striving for universal knowledge, especially for painters. "A painter is not admirable unless he is universal,"[1] he said. He went on to explain that painters seek to reproduce any and all of the creatures and objects of the natural world on their canvases, so they should study and become an expert on as many of those things as possible. He stated,

> Since we know that painting embraces and includes in itself every object produced by nature or resulting from the fortuitous actions of men, in short, all that the eye can see, he seems to me but a poor master who can only do a figure well. For do you not perceive how many and various actions are performed by men only; how many different animals there are, as well as trees, plants, flowers, with many mountainous regions and plains, springs and rivers, cities with public and private buildings, machines, too, fit for the purposes of men, [diverse] costumes, decorations and arts? And all these things ought to be regarded as of equal importance and value, by the man who can be termed a good painter.[2]

"Large and Magnificent Tasks"

Leonardo was not the first or only European to stress the importance of universal knowledge and strive for it. He admired and modeled himself on the great Italian architect Leon Battista Alberti, who died in 1472 when Leonardo was 20. Alberti designed buildings, painted, sculpted, composed music, designed machines to raise sunken ships, and wrote a play in Latin and the leading Renaissance book on architecture. In addition, he was a gifted athlete who some claimed could leap over a standing adult in a single bound. Alberti wrote, "Man is born ... to work at large and magnificent tasks, thereby pleasing and honoring God, and manifesting in himself perfect virtue, that is, the fruit of happiness."[3]

Leonardo wanted to create his own "fruit of happiness" by investigating, studying, and in some cases, mastering a wide variety of subjects including painting, sculpture, music, architecture, mathematics, engineering, human anatomy, cartography (mapmaking), and botany (studies of plant life). People were amazed at his versatility. Indeed, he appeared to be the greatest among the polymaths who flourished within the remarkable intellectual and artistic realm of Renaissance society.

The Italian painter and historian Giorgio Vasari was one of many noted observers of the age who commented on Leonardo's gifts. In his biography of Leonardo, which remains one of the key sources of information about him, Vasari wrote,

> Sometimes, in supernatural fashion, beauty, grace, and talent are united beyond measure in one single person, in a manner that to whatever such an one turns his attention, his every action is so divine, that, surpassing all other men, it makes itself clearly known as a thing bestowed by God ... This was seen by all mankind in Leonardo da Vinci.[4]

Renaissance Rock Star

Time has not diminished Leonardo's high stature in the public consciousness of Western civilization. Leonardo's most famous work, the *Mona Lisa*, remains an object of fascination and wonder. "No other painting in the world has been reproduced as often," author Serge Bramly wrote. "No other attracts as many visitors or has been 'borrowed' by so many other artists."[5] By the middle of the 19th century, art scholar Roy McMullen wrote, the *Mona Lisa* had become "a goal for pilgrimages and the object of a cult [of rabid fans]. It is decidedly not just a painting like other paintings. It might be better described ... as a cross between a universal fetish [craze] and a Hollywood era film star."[6]

If the *Mona Lisa* can be designated a movie star, its creator would best be described as one of the rock stars of the fine arts world (along with his fellow Italian Michelangelo and a handful of others). Leonardo is still as big an object of wonder as his renowned, or famous, painting. He is also a source of mystery. Various writers and conspiracy theorists have claimed that he hid secret codes in his paintings and notebooks. Such theories have spawned numerous books and movies, which have contributed to making Leonardo a household name around the globe among people of all ages.

The primary public fascination with Leonardo, however, centers on the fact of his genius and versatility as an artist, thinker, and inventor. In scholar Stefan Klein's words,

> How could one individual fuse within himself what appeared to be the knowledge of the entire world? ... How was he able to create epoch-making paintings—and at the same time immerse himself in designing flying machines, robots, and all kinds of other devices and in contemplating a broad range of scientific questions? It seems miraculous that any one person could make his mark in so many areas in the course of a lifetime.[7]

No other painting in the history of art has gathered the same amount of attention and fascination as the Mona Lisa.

This engraving of Leonardo by Cosomo Colombini shows the artist in good health and strong spirits.

The reasons Leonardo managed to accomplish so much in one lifetime are a matter of speculation and will likely remain a mystery. Glimpses into his motivation are sometimes spotted in his surviving writings. Some indicate that he disliked the idea of wasting time. To not put all of one's talents and energies to work at all times was, in Leonardo's opinion, a guarantee that you would not leave a mark on the world and be quickly forgotten after you died. According to one of his apprentices, Leonardo once said, "He who … burns his life to waste leaves no more vestige of himself on earth than wind-blown smoke, or the foam upon the sea."[8] Leonardo certainly listened to his own advice. As a person and an artist, he left a huge mark on the world, and because of that, he will never be forgotten.

CHAPTER ONE

A Man Like No Other

Leonardo da Vinci was born on April 15, 1452, in a small hill town called Vinci, then part of the territory of the northern Italian city-state of Florence. His father, Piero Fruosino di Antonio da Vinci, was a landlord and notary (a person who certifies legal documents). His mother was a peasant woman named Caterina. Leonardo's unmarried parents did not stay together, and both married other people before their son's first birthday.

In 1939, a researcher discovered a note about Leonardo's birth in Florence's official archives. Written by Leonardo's grandfather, Antonio, it read in part, "1452: There was born to me a grandson, the son of ... Piero my son, on the 15th day of April, a Saturday, at the third hour of the night. He bears the name Leonardo."[9] Like his father and grandfather, the baby received no last name. The words "da Vinci" mean simply "from Vinci" or "of Vinci." That means he is generally referred to as Leonardo instead of being called by a last name as is traditionally done.

An Early Education

Almost nothing is known about Leonardo's childhood. He never wrote of his early years, perhaps because he had been an illegitimate child and did not want anyone to know. For the first four or five years of his life, Leonardo lived with his mother and stepfather, who had moved to Campo Zeppi, a hamlet within walking distance of Vinci.

After that, for obscure reasons, Leonardo went to live with his father and stepmother in his grandfather's house in Vinci. He was likely taught by female relatives and an occasional tutor. Although he was not taught Latin, which most formal schools endlessly drilled into their students, he did learn mathematics—something he would use quite a bit in the coming years.

At some point in his youth, Leonardo shared his passion for drawing with his father. According to biographer Giorgio Vasari, Leonardo never stopped drawing the things around him. His father, impressed with what he saw, took the drawings to Florentine sculptor and painter Andrea del Verrocchio. Verrocchio ran a successful studio and regularly took in and trained apprentices. Leonardo's father asked Verrocchio if his son might one day make a living as an artist if he stuck with it. In Vasari's words, the sculptor "was astonished" at the boy's talent and "urged Ser Piero that he should make him study it."[10]

At age 14, Leonardo became Verrocchio's apprentice. For a young man accustomed to life in villages and small towns, the move to Florence, one of Italy's busiest and most attractive cities, must have been exciting. Adding to the thrill, no doubt, was the fact that he would now receive formal training in a number of trades and disciplines, including plaster casting, metalworking, carpentry, drawing, painting, and sculpture. "As an apprentice," researcher Robert Wallace explained,

Leonardo doubtless followed the standard routine, commencing with the grinding of colors [paint pigments] and other drudgery and then, as his skills increased, gradually being allowed to execute the simpler parts of whatever work Verrocchio happened to have in hand. Much of what he learned must have come from the master himself, but there were more advanced pupils or assistants in the shop, notably Pietro Perugino, six years older than Leonardo, from whom he may have learned basic techniques. In his turn, Leonardo obviously helped and influenced younger apprentices, such as Lorenzo di Credi, whose style eventually became so slavishly 'Leonardoesque' that it sometimes requires an expert eye to tell their works apart.[11]

The nature of most of the projects Leonardo worked on with Verrocchio is uncertain. However, a few of these projects have been identified by modern experts. One of these projects includes some work done by Leonardo on Verrocchio's painting *Tobias and the Angel.*

Even from a young age, Leonardo drew with incredible detail.

Leonardo

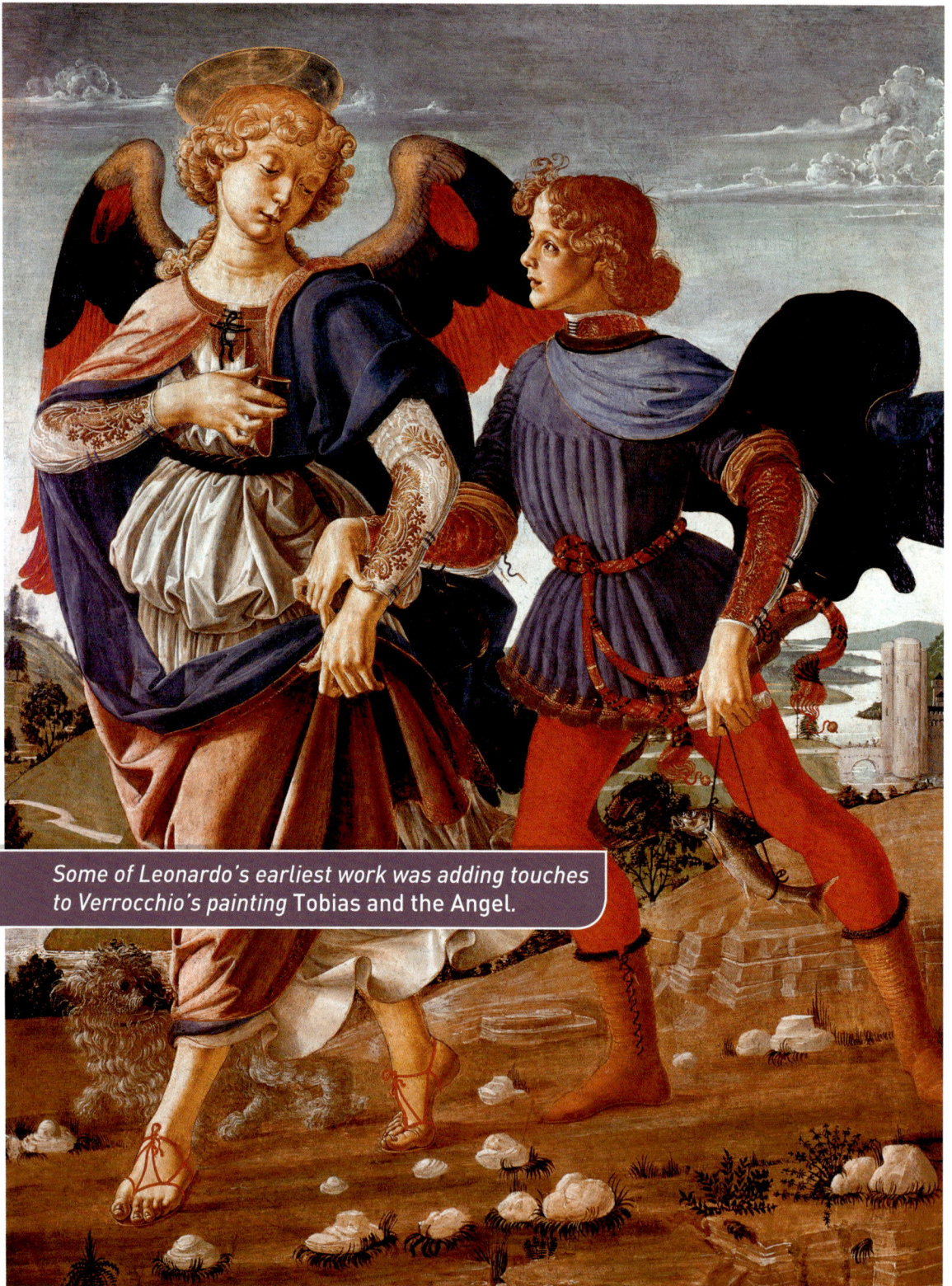

Some of Leonardo's earliest work was adding touches to Verrocchio's painting Tobias and the Angel.

In those days, as Wallace wrote, major artists allowed their leading apprentices to work on small sections of the works their studios turned out. It is now generally accepted that Leonardo painted the fish held by Tobias in the picture and maybe the dog running next to the angel.

Eventually, Verrocchio allowed Leonardo to tackle more challenging projects. Sometime in his late teens, according to Vasari, Leonardo painted substantial parts of Verrocchio's *Baptism of Christ*. The younger man's brushstrokes are indeed recognizable in the figure of the kneeling angel and in much of the figure of Jesus as well. In addition, some evidence suggests that Verrocchio may have sometimes used Leonardo, who is said to have been a handsome youth, as a model. A number of art historians think that the face of Verrocchio's statue of the biblical character David was fashioned after that of his star apprentice.

The Status of Master

Leonardo showed so much promise that by 1472, at the age of 20, both his father and his painting master felt he was ready to strike out on his own. He was granted the status of master, or skilled professional, by Florence's prestigious Guild of St. Luke, an organization of independent artists. Piero da Vinci arranged for his talented son to have his own workshop, but Leonardo felt more comfortable continuing to work on projects with his close friend and mentor Verrocchio. It was not until 1478 that the younger artist began accepting major commissions for artworks on his own.

The first of these independent projects was the creation of an altarpiece, or decoration for a church altar, for Florence's Chapel of St. Bernard (which he never fully conceptualized or finished). He also began work on a large wooden panel painting for the monastery of San Donato a Scopeto in 1481. Titled *The Adoration of the Magi*, its subject was the infant Jesus in his manger accompanied by his mother, Mary. Unlike most painted manger scenes, which are small-scale and intimate, Leonardo's was large-scale and busy, with dozens of shepherds, visitors, angels, and other figures milling about behind the mother and child, including a shepherd whose face is likely a self-portrait of the artist.

The work was not finished, however, because in 1482, Leonardo abruptly left Florence and journeyed to Milan, 155 miles (249 km) to the northwest. Another bustling Italian center of trade and the arts, Milan was then ruled by Duke Ludovico Sforza (also known as Ludovico il Moro), an autocratic leader but dedicated patron of the arts. It is not completely clear why Leonardo moved, but he accepted the post of official artist for the duke's court.

Verrocchio may have used Leonardo as a model for his statue of David. Leonardo's handsome face and curly hair may have inspired a number of other artists to use him as a model, too.

Perhaps Leonardo hoped the huge financial backing and prestige of the Sforza family would provide him with opportunities he could not find elsewhere. He also may have been attracted by rumors that Milan's ruler was looking for someone to create an enormous sculpture of a horse. Landing such an assignment was guaranteed to make any artist famous and in demand throughout Europe.

To get the desired post in Ludovico's court, Leonardo composed a letter much like a modern-day resume. Clearly intended to impress the duke, it claimed that the applicant was capable of much more than just painting pretty pictures. It was well known that the duke was not only an arts supporter, but also a military man interested in expanding Milan's influence, if necessary, by force. So Leonardo stressed that he was capable of fashioning all manner of effective defensive and offensive weapons, including cannons, smoke machines, and armored vehicles. He said in part,

> I have [invented] many machines most efficient for [military] offense and defense, and vessels which will resist the attack of the largest guns and powder and fumes … In case of [your] need, I will make big guns, mortars, [but] where the operation of bombardment might fail, I would contrive catapults … In time of peace I … [can design] buildings, public and private …

> I can carry out sculpture in marble, bronze, or clay, and also I can do in painting whatever may [need to] be done … If any of the above-mentioned things seem to anyone to be impossible … I am most ready to [demonstrate them] in whatever place may please your Excellency.[12]

Notes for the Mirror

Painting, sculpture, architecture, and military engineering were not the only talents and services that Leonardo could offer Ludovico. The gifted young man was also a capable writer and musician. Leonardo kept a huge mass of detailed notes, and centuries later, they were collected and published as his notebooks. The notes ranged from brilliant plans to grocery lists and jokes. He composed most of these notes using "mirror writing," in which he wrote backward, requiring one to look at the writing in a mirror to read it. The reason for this approach was different than many people today assume. According to Martin Clayton, an expert on Leonardo's work, the artist was

> left-handed, and throughout his life he habitually wrote these notes in mirror-image, from right to left. This was not an attempt to keep his researches secret, as has been claimed, for Leonardo's mirror-writing is relatively easy to

Although Leonardo's handwriting (shown here) seems strange, to him it seemed like a natural way for a left-handed person to write.

read with a little patience. Mirror-writing is a common developmental quirk in childhood, and what may have begun as an entertaining trick became a habit that Leonardo never had cause to discard.[13]

Leonardo also learned to use mirrors to help him become a better judge or critic of his own paintings while he was working on them. He explained in his notes:

We know very well that errors are better recognised in the works of others than in our own; and that often, while [finding] little faults in others, you may ignore great ones in yourself. To avoid such ignorance ... I say that when you paint you should have a flat mirror and often look at your work as reflected in it, when you will see it reversed, and it will appear to you like some other painter's work, so you will be better able to judge of its faults than in any other way.[14]

In addition, Leonardo somehow found the time to learn to play several musical instruments, including the lyre, a small harp popular in ancient and medieval times. He also designed a number of new instruments, including some flutelike devices and a complex keyboard instrument with strings. One of his instruments, the viola organista, was "a complex instrument that permitted the bowing of many strings through the control of a keyboard, and therefore allowed ten fingers to produce the tone of a whole little orchestra of viols."[15]

Under the Duke's Sponsorship

Leonardo ended up living and working in Milan from 1482 to 1499. During this time, he was almost constantly busy. Although his official role was that of court painter, Ludovico employed him on many other projects. Among them were designing elaborate decorations for feasts and weddings held by the duke and his leading nobles and helping to plan new additions to the Milan Cathedral (the Duomo di Milano). Ludovico also assigned Leonardo to the creation of a giant equine (horse-shaped) statue, proving the earlier rumors true.

While drawing sketches for the great statue's design and working on a clay model, Leonardo also spent much of his time engaging in his chief profession—painting. The first major painting he did under Duke Ludovico's sponsorship was his initial version of *The Virgin of the Rocks* (sometimes translated to *The Madonna of the Rocks*). Completed in 1486, it is nearly identical to a second version the artist began in Milan in 1495. (The reason he did two separate versions remains unclear.) Leonardo also painted a large mural

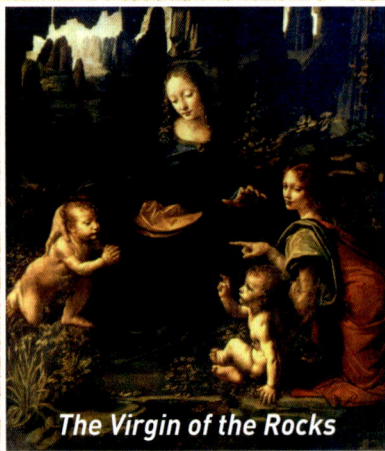

The Virgin of the Rocks

A Salute to the Memory

Late author Robert Payne wrote about Leonardo's humanity, pointing out how thoughtful and courteous he was to people, even the dead and those he did not know well or at all:

An old man, a centenarian [someone 100 years old or older], died in the hospital where [Leonardo] was working. Leonardo talked to him during his last hours and discovered that he had never had a day's illness. Immediately after the man died, Leonardo [who had obtained the man's permission to dissect him after his death] began to cut him up in the hope of learning what changes in the physical body bring about death. At the top of the first page of his anatomical study of the old man, he drew, with grave courtesy, a portrait of the man as he was when alive. It was Leonardo's salute to the memory of the living man, while he was engaged in dismembering the corpse. His life was made up of such acts of courtesy.[1]

1. Robert Payne, *Leonardo: His Life and Works*. Garden City, NY: Doubleday, 1978, p. xvi.

for Ludovico—*The Last Supper*, finished in 1498, which became one of the artist's two most famous works.

Not long after completing *The Last Supper*, Leonardo was forced to leave Milan. In 1499, Duke Ludovico was defeated by an invading French army, which seized control of the city. Leonardo fled to Venice, in northeastern Italy, and in the following year, he returned to his native Florence. There he was greeted as a celebrity and provided with a spacious workshop by the monks of a local monastery. According to Vasari, that workshop was where Leonardo did the cartoon, or preliminary full-sized drawing, for an ultimately unfinished painting titled *The Virgin and Child with St. Anne.* (Some modern experts think Vasari was wrong and that the cartoon was done shortly before the artist left Milan.)

In 1502, Leonardo headed to Cesena, about halfway between Florence and Venice. There he entered the service of Cesare Borgia, son of Pope Alexander VI and a member of a notorious family of political schemers. As a military engineer for his new boss, Leonardo traveled widely through the Italian peninsula. Borgia was extremely impressed with him and trusted him with important assignments, including inspecting and maintaining the several Borgia-controlled forts.

A surviving document signed by Borgia gave Leonardo safe passage to carry out his inspections. It reads in part:

> Our most excellent and well-beloved friend, the architect and engineer ... Leonardo Vinci ... shall be given free passage and be relieved of all public tax, both for himself and his party, and shall be welcomed amicably, and may make measurements and examine whatever he pleases ... It is our will that every engineer in our dominions shall be bound to confer with him and follow his advice. And let no man dare to do the contrary, if he does not wish to incur our extreme displeasure.[16]

Ahead of His Time

In 1503, for reasons unknown, Leonardo left Borgia's employ and went back to Florence. There, the artist worked on a huge mural—*The Battle of Anghiari*, yet another project he left unfinished. It appears that he also began working on the *Mona Lisa*, by far his most renowned artwork, around this time.

By 1508, Leonardo had moved back to Milan. At age 56, he found himself devoting more and more time to his scientific studies in botany, mechanics, the nature of flight, and human anatomy, which he had focused on intermittently during most of his adult life. Every conclusion and theory Leonardo reached, he backed up with numerous elaborate and detailed drawings. Some illustrations show primitive helicopters and glider planes, parachutes, battleships, submarines, steam-powered weapons, and what appear to be robots— all devices centuries ahead of their time. Perhaps the most impressive of Leonardo's sketches were his anatomical renderings. According to the late Sherwin B. Nuland, who was a medical historian,

> No one before him ... made so many dissections on human bodies, nor did any understand so well how to interpret the findings. His account of the uterus was far more accurate ... than any that preceded him. He was the first to give a correct description of the human skeleton ... of the vertebral column, [and] practically all the muscles of the human body. No one before him had drawn the nerves and the blood vessels even approximately as correctly as he ... nor had anyone before him [drawn] that wealth of anatomical details which he observed.[17]

In 1513, Giuliano de' Medici, brother of Pope Leo X, invited Leonardo to live and work in the Vatican, the pope's residence in Rome. Not much is known about what Leonardo did there, but most

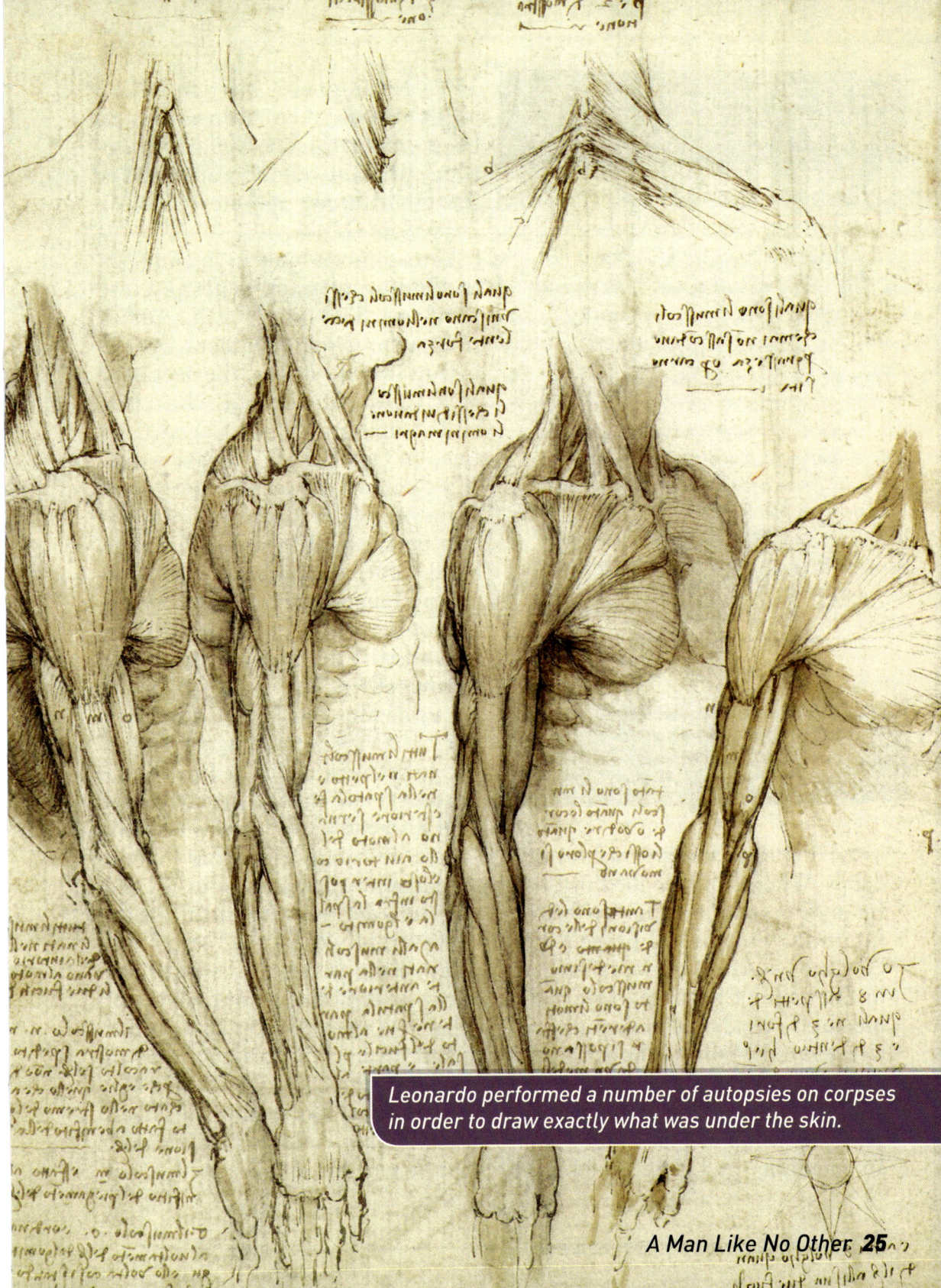

Leonardo performed a number of autopsies on corpses in order to draw exactly what was under the skin.

CHAPTER TWO

The Beginning Artist

Leonardo was brilliant and accomplished in so many ways, but he was, foremost, a painter. He was a very slow painter, and he often did not finish what he had started. Still, he managed to create some of history's most famous paintings, such as the *Mona Lisa* and *The Last Supper*. He also had an impact on many other artists—both in his time and today. Art experts have identified fewer than 20 paintings that can definitely be attributed to Leonardo's hand. The fact that his huge reputation as a painter rests mainly on only a few works speaks volumes about his nearly unmatched artistic inventiveness and skill.

Why did Leonardo leave so many of his paintings unfinished? There are several reasons, but the primary one is the large amount of time he invested in planning and preparing for each project, including conducting research and creating numerous preliminary sketches and notes. According to Bramly,

Leonardo's well-known slowness and the small number of his works were the result ... of the trouble he took over the conception of each work. He never began a painting until he had thoroughly mastered his subject. He was incapable of repeating what had already been done by someone else, and only took up his brushes once a revolution in the mind had been

This portrait of 16-year-old poet Ginevra de' Benci demonstrates Leonardo's ability to show facial expression.

accomplished. A radical innovator, a thinker, and a perfectionist, he left infinitely more studies and notes than any other Renaissance artist.[21]

Leonardo's paintings were and remain remarkable for their striking portrayal of the human form. This can be seen in the works he did in his first broad painting period, before 1490, and his later one, which encompassed the years afterward. His characters almost always seem to be filled with an inner energy and display distinct emotional expressions. These attributes are most famously associated with the *Mona Lisa* but can be seen in his other paintings, too. As noted art historian Elke Linda Buchholz wrote, "His compositions produce an extraordinarily lively effect and appear harmonic and flowing. Typically, Leonardo created very fine modulations [variations] of light and shadow, especially with faces and background landscapes. His human beings express finely differentiated feelings. In creating these figures, he always strove for ideal beauty."[22]

Following His Own Path

The expert use of light and shadow and straightforward depiction of the inner feelings of human subjects are clearly visible even in Leonardo's earliest paintings, especially in *The Baptism of Christ*. Produced by Verrocchio's studio,

The Baptism of Christ was commissioned around 1470 by the monks of the San Salvi monastery, just outside of Florence. The painting shows Jesus wearing a loincloth, standing in the center with two angels kneeling to his right. Jesus's cousin, John the Baptist, is on his left, anointing Jesus's head with water from the Jordan River.

Modern experts have closely studied the work, analyzing its unique brushstrokes and subtle uses of color and light. Their consensus is that Verrocchio painted an initial version of the work using tempera. Around this time, many European painters used this type of paint, made by mixing powdered pigments with egg yolk, water, or some other liquid and a small amount of glue to make sure the paint would stick to the painting surface.

Thanks to extensive experiments by a few inventive Dutch artists, however, oil-based paints rapidly supplanted tempera. Dutchman Jan van Eyck perfected the oil-painting medium and demonstrated that using oil allowed an artist to produce more intricate detail than was possible with tempera. This was because oil paint takes longer to dry, so a painter has considerably more time to add detail or make changes.

Although it is difficult to tell for sure, the transition from tempera to oil seems to have occurred in Verrocchio's workshop in the

The contrast between the two angels in the painting makes it clear that more than one artist worked on The Baptism of Christ.

early 1470s, and around 1472, *The Baptism of Christ* painting underwent a facelift. Most of the work, which had been painted in tempera on a wooden panel, was painted over with oils. It also appears that Leonardo was responsible for many of the additions. Experts can recognize his unique brushwork in several sections of the picture. In particular, the angel at the far left in the revised version is completely Leonardo's and quite different in appearance from Verrocchio's version. According to the BBC, "We believe that the angel on the left, and much of the background above it, were painted by a young Leonardo. Most of the painting is done in egg tempera, but Leonardo's angel is painted with oil paints, which were just being introduced to Italy. X-rays show that this part of the painting differs significantly from Verrocchio's original sketches."[23]

The other sections of the painting that Leonardo redid in oils included parts of Jesus's body, including his torso and the heavy eyelids that give his face such a poignant expression. Leonardo also "radically altered the landscape in the distance," art historian Jack Wasserman wrote. He "brought the water forward from the middle ground so that it eddies around Christ's feet. In so doing, he had perhaps hoped to disguise

the [disjointed break] between the middle distance and the foreground of the [original] painting, thereby unifying them."[24]

From Helping Out to on His Own

Leonardo contributed to other painting projects while working in Verrocchio's studio in the 1470s. One that has been verified as partially his

is part of a two-piece work titled *The Annunciation* produced by the studio in that decade. In Christian religious traditions, the Annunciation is the moment when the angel Gabriel tells the biblical Mary that she will soon conceive a divine child. Both versions of the painting created by Verrocchio's assistants show the angel kneeling on the left-hand side of the painting, reaching out with his right hand toward Mary, who sits on the right. They are on a stone terrace that overlooks a distant landscape of small seaports filled with ships.

One of the two paintings, now in the Louvre Museum in Paris, France, is clearly not Leonardo's, and experts still debate which of Verrocchio's helpers executed it. The other work, which hangs in Florence's Uffizi Gallery, was, for a long time,

The Annunciation *was created by numerous artists who tried to blend their work to look like a single style.*

Despite being unfinished, the people in Leonardo's The Adoration of the Magi *clearly display a wide range and depth of emotions, including wonder, curiosity, devotion, joy, and contemplation.*

attributed to another painter but has since been shown to be partly done by Leonardo. The expert consensus is that Leonardo contributed the overall design and painted parts of the angel and all the background landscape. The rest of the picture seems to have been done by other members of Verrocchio's studio.

The first major painting Leonardo attempted on his own was *The Adoration of the Magi*, commissioned in 1481 by the monastery of San Donato a Scopeto. Leonardo never finished the work. All that has survived on the original wooden panel is a monochromatic (colorless or single-colored) initial drawing, to which the artist intended to add paint. Still, it is more than a mere cartoon. Leonardo took the next step beyond line drawing and blocked in most of the light and shadowed areas, giving much of the panel a three-dimensional look.

The most striking aspect of the work is the controlled chaos, so to speak, of the masses of human figures surrounding Jesus and Mary, who dominate the center foreground. In addition to the Magi (the three foreign kings bearing gifts for Jesus), there are shepherds, soldiers, angels, and other figures. No painter before Leonardo had tried to portray so many varied emotions in a single painting. One scholar wrote that Leonardo was the only artist who recognized the potential of showing numerous "powerful and identifiable emotions and raised them to such a level of universality that they inspire in the beholder comparable feelings of awe and devotion."[25]

Another important aspect of *The Adoration of the Magi* is Leonardo's depiction of horses. They can be seen running and rearing up in the background as their riders engage in jousting matches. For years before beginning this work, Leonardo had been fascinated by horses and had studied and sketched them standing, walking, trotting, and rearing up on their hind legs. No other Renaissance artist surpassed him in representing horses. Moreover, no other artist of the period could match him in capturing the look, dynamics, and tensions of combat, both with and without horses.

Another Unfinished Project

Evidence suggests that Leonardo began work on *The Adoration of the Magi* sometime between 1481 and 1482, shortly before he left Florence to work for Duke Ludovico in Milan. It was not the only painting that he left unfinished from that short time. He also started, but did not complete, a panel painting portraying the well-known biblical character St. Jerome. Like *The Adoration of the Magi*, *St. Jerome* has survived as a brownish monochromatic drawing in which most of the shading had been added in preparation for adding the colored pigments.

Despite its lack of full color, the composition and figures in *St. Jerome* are clear enough to show that it is one of Leonardo's most dramatic scenes. As Payne described it:

We see St. Jerome kneeling beside a lion, one arm out-flung, gazing penitently and adoringly at a crucifix. He is naked except for a cloak falling loosely over his left shoulder. He is very old and the deeply lined face and emaciated [very thin] body have the dignity of age. Behind him lies the desert with the strange bulbous rocks that [also] appear in the Adoration of the Magi in the distance, while closer at hand ... is a heap of rocks and what appears to be the entrance of a grotto [cave] where the saint spent the better part of his life. One imagines that a cry has just escaped from the saint's lips. The lion's mouth is open, and he is roaring.[26]

The gaunt figure of St. Jerome reflects Leonardo's studies in human anatomy, which he had recently begun. Among other things, his studies involved creating detailed drawings of body parts he observed during the dissection of corpses.

St. Jerome's Fate

Leonardo's painting of *St. Jerome*, one of his most dramatic and popular works, underwent a torturous existence in the centuries following its creator's death. For a while it was kept safe at the Vatican, the home and office of the Catholic pope. Later, the artwork passed into the possession of a woman named Angelica Kauffmann. After Kauffman's death, the painting was lost, and an unknown individual, not realizing its worth, cut it into five pieces. One section became a box cover, and a shoemaker used the other section as part of a stool. Still other pieces were used on a workbench. A Catholic cardinal named Joseph Fesch recognized the painting on the box cover and stool in 1820. Over time, he managed to find the other pieces, and the painting was restored. After Fesch's death, the piece was purchased by Pope Pius IX in 1856. Today, *St. Jerome* can be found in the Vatican in Rome, Italy.

In this manner, the young man had become quite familiar with the bones and muscles of the body, and some of what he had learned can be seen in Jerome's almost skeletal appearance.

The saint's figure is reminiscent not only of Leonardo's anatomical drawings, but also of other sketches he had been doing of disfigured or odd-looking people or a mixture of both that he sometimes encountered on street corners and elsewhere. Vasari referred to Leonardo's interest in the bizarre, saying that he was

> *so delighted when he saw curious[-looking human] heads ... that he would follow about anyone who had thus attracted his attention for a whole day, acquiring such a clear idea of him that when he went home he would draw the head as well as if the man had been present. In this way, many heads of men and women came to be drawn, and I have several such pen-and-ink drawings in my [possession].*[27]

Another important aspect of *St. Jerome* is the lion in the foreground. Several art historians and critics have remarked over the years that in spite of its lack of detail in the preliminary drawing, the image is sleek, well-proportioned, and very believable. There was a good reason for this expertise in depicting lions. Although the horse may well have been Leonardo's favorite beast, he also had a strong interest in many other animals, especially lions. His admiration for lions and what he perceived as their courage can be seen in a remark from his notebooks: "The lion is never afraid, but rather fights with a bold spirit and savage onslaught against a multitude of hunters, always seeking to injure the first that injures him."[28]

Leonardo visited and studied several lions that were kept in a lion house in Florence during his childhood and early adulthood. During a nostalgic moment when he was in his 60s, he drew the lion house from memory. His notebooks also contain a reference to lions in captivity that he may have learned about firsthand: "We see the most striking example of humility in the lamb which will submit to any animal; and when they are given for food to imprisoned lions they are as gentle to them as to their own mother, so that very often it has been seen that the lions forbear to kill them."[29]

Baffling Imagery and Unanswered Questions

St. Jerome also contains an interesting visual metaphor involving lions. In the wild, the now extinct European species of lions were known to sometimes dwell in caves. The fact that Jerome also lived in a cave, which the artist included in the picture, gives the saint a sort of shared brotherhood with the beast.

The inclusion of a lion in St. Jerome *reminds viewers that Leonardo found the creatures fascinating and powerful.*

Another major painting from the first two decades of Leonardo's artistic career depicts a cave. Frequently called his most original painting, as well as his strangest and most puzzling work, it is titled *The Virgin of the Rocks* (sometimes translated into English as *The Madonna of the Rocks*). It dates to between 1483 and 1486, which means it was created during Leonardo's early years in Milan. "The painting is a mysterious revelation," author Robert Wallace wrote, "with a setting that is not of this earth, a watery cave, open to the sky, sheltering the Virgin [Mary], the infants [Jesus] and John [the Baptist], and an angel … The figures are supremely graceful and at ease, and the details of plant life are as true to nature as the most skilled botanical artist could draw them."[30]

The painting is indeed baffling in its unusual imagery, most of it apparently symbolic. Why, for instance, does the angel point emphatically at baby John rather than at Jesus? Is the child whom Mary touches with her right hand really John after all? Might he instead be a representation of humanity in general, which the New Testament of the Bible says Jesus saved by dying on the cross? People have also conjectured that the cave might be symbolic of a mystical womb, since Jesus had recently come from Mary's womb through divine intervention.

No one has ever been able to answer these and other such questions about *The Virgin of the Rocks*. Robert Wallace pointed out that Leonardo, "like most great painters, never made the slightest effort to explain this or any other of his works."[31] One possible explanation of Leonardo's use of the cave that scholars have offered is that he was long haunted by an experience he had had in a real cave when he was a young man. Leonardo described part of this experience in a passage from his notebooks, writing,

Having wandered some distance among gloomy rocks, I came to the entrance of a great cavern, in front of which I stood some time, astonished and unaware of such a thing. Bending my back into an arch I rested my left hand on my knee and held my right hand over my down-cast and contracted eye brows. Often bending first one way and then the other, to see whether I could discover anything inside, and this being forbidden by the deep darkness within, and after having remained there some time, two contrary emotions arose in me, fear and desire—fear of the threatening dark cavern, desire to see whether there were any marvelous thing within it.[32]

The setting of **The Virgin of the Rocks** *was very unusual for a portrayal of Mary.*

A Mysterious Glance

Many art critics and historians have described Leonardo's *The Virgin of the Rocks* over the centuries. One of the more effective descriptions of the painting was by biographer Antonina Vallentin:

A strange darkness fills the grotto in which the Virgin is kneeling. Shadows play amid the dank and trickling cliffs, and the plants and stones glisten mysteriously in the velvety hollow, which suddenly opens out to admit the entrance of light in the far distance. These rocky ledges that overhang the darkness of the hollow, this medley of flowers springing from the rich moss, might equally well be the resting-place of heathen gods. Light-footed nymphs might emerge in alarm from the golden twilight, fleeing from the god Pan in this enchanted wilderness. There is more, too, of a heathen god than a heavenly messenger in the angel who has come down by the side of the Christ Child, the flaming red stain of his garment spreading out as he suddenly kneels. An ecstatic [thrilled] glance comes from his almond-shaped eyes between their fleshy and sensual lids, a glance laden with mystery.[1]

1. Antonina Vallentin, *Leonardo da Vinci: The Tragic Pursuit of Perfection*. Trans. by E. W. Dicks. New York, NY: Viking, 1938, pp. 97–98.

What Leonardo intended the cave, the pointing finger, and other visual images to represent in *The Virgin of the Rocks* will likely never be known. It was Leonardo's last major painting before his death in 1519. For most artists, past and present, turning out a painting as finely wrought as *The Virgin of the Rocks*, or even the unfinished *Adoration of the Magi*, would be enough to create a major reputation. However, Leonardo was destined for greater things.

A Restless Mind

Beginning in the 1490s, Leonardo managed to outdo his younger self by producing some of the most sublime and famous artworks of all time. By always carrying a notebook with him, he was able to write lists and draw whatever thoughts or concepts came to mind right away. He once wrote, "It is useful ... to constantly observe, note, and consider."[33] In one of his notebooks dating around the 1490s, researchers discovered a "to do" list. Not all of what Leonardo listed can be clearly understood today, but still the list is daunting. It contains more than a dozen items, including "[Calculate] the measurement of Milan and Suburbs," "Get the master of arithmetic to show you how to square a triangle," and "Find a master of hydraulics and get him to tell you how to repair a lock, canal and mill in the Lombard manner."[34] This list makes it clear that while Leonardo was producing amazing artwork, his mind was constantly thinking and calculating and wondering about everything else around him. His was truly the world of a polymath.

CHAPTER THREE

New Techniques, New Masterpieces

Leonardo accomplished quite a lot by 1490, but some of his best work was yet to come. Between 1490 and 1513, he shifted locations several times. In 1490, he was still working with Duke Ludovico, but then he moved to his home city of Florence in 1503. He stayed there for five years before returning to Milan in 1508. During these years, Leonardo started a number of paintings that were never finished; however, those pictures he did complete—*The Last Supper*, the *Mona Lisa*, and *Salvator Mundi*—are considered among the greatest paintings in art history.

In an effort to make his works appear more realistic, Leonardo kept experimenting with new ideas and approaches. This resulted in the development of two techniques that revolutionized the art of painting.

First, young Leonardo noticed that the farther away an object is from a viewer, the more its hue shifts toward the blue end of the spectrum. (This is because over a distance Earth's atmosphere variously absorbs and scatters the colors making up white light.) Leonardo also noticed that over a distance, the atmosphere appears increasingly hazy. His depiction of these atmospheric effects in his background landscapes became known as aerial perspective.

The second important technique Leonardo developed is called sfumato (from the Italian word *sfumare*, meaning "to tone down"). It is, as one expert said, "a fine, almost unnoticeable blur found especially over facial features, but also over landscapes. In this way, Leonardo avoided the over-sharp precision and stiffness of earlier portraiture. Tones blend into one another, and the landscape melds with the human figure, the cosmos with humanity."[35] Leonardo used these and other techniques to great effect in a number of his later works, with particularly stunning results in his masterpieces the Mona Lisa and The Last Supper.

The Restoration

The Last Supper, which depicts the final meal shared by Jesus and his 12 disciples, was requested by Duke Ludovico. He wanted it to adorn the north wall of the refectory, or dining hall, of Milan's Church of Santa Maria delle Grazie, which was to be his burial place. The plan was for an unusually large mural, measuring 29 feet by 15 feet (8.8 m by 4.6 m), which would clearly be a challenge for any painter. Rising to that challenge, Leonardo, who was a perfectionist, spent nearly three years doing preliminary studies and drawings. He began applying the paint in 1495 and completed the mural in late 1497 or early 1498. An eyewitness account of the actual creation of this renowned picture has survived. Italian writer Matteo Bandello visited the dining hall on several occasions as the work progressed and later recalled,

[Leonardo] would often come to the [church] at early dawn. And this I have seen him do myself. Hastily mounting the scaffolding, he worked diligently until the shades of evening compelled him to cease, never thinking to take food at all, so absorbed was he in his work. At other times he would remain there three or four days without touching his picture, only coming for a few hours to remain before it, with folded arms, gazing at his figures as if to criticize them himself. At midday, too, when the glare of the sun at its zenith has made barren all the streets of Milan, I have seen him hasten from the citadel, where he was [working on a sculpture for the duke], without seeking the shade, by the shortest way to the [church], where he would add a touch or two [to the painting] and immediately return [to the citadel].[36]

The seemingly endless days of hard work that Bandello witnessed paid off. The monks were amazed by the degree of realism Leonardo had imparted to the figures in the picture, as were all others who saw it in its original state. Everyone agreed that the painting also beautifully captured the emotions of the men portrayed as they realized that one of the apostles was going to betray Jesus. Vasari, who viewed the mural only a few years after the artist's death, wrote,

Leonardo imagined and succeeded in expressing that anxiety which had seized the Apostles in wishing to know who should betray their Master. For that reason, in all their faces are seen love, fear, and wrath, or rather, sorrow, at not being able to understand the meaning of Christ ... not to mention that every least part of the work displays an incredible diligence, seeing that even in the tablecloth the texture of the stuff is [painted] in such a manner that linen itself could not seem more real.[37]

Regrettably, Vasari also noticed that the picture's paint was already beginning to fade and chip away. The chief culprit was moisture, as the combination of tempera and oil that Leonardo had employed proved unable to withstand the room's high humidity. He had not been trained in the fresco technique of painting on the wet plaster of a wall or ceiling, so he chose painting materials poorly. To make matters worse, as the colors continued to fade, the painting suffered one added humiliation after another. According to the BBC,

[The poor choice of materials], along with the humid conditions in the [church], meant that the painting began deteriorating while Leonardo was still alive. The refectory has also been flooded and used as a stable—but the painting's luckiest escape came during the Second World War, when the refectory was hit by a bomb. Only some carefully placed sandbags saved this masterpiece from destruction.[38]

A number of attempts were made over the centuries to repair *The Last Supper*. Most of these attempts were inadequate, and some made the existing damage to the painting even worse. Another valiant effort was completed in 1954 by master art restorer Mauro Pellicioli. In 1978, Italian authorities decided the painting needed yet another restoration attempt and hired art restorer Pinin Brambilla Barcilon for the job. It was an overwhelming project that lasted 20 years. In 1999, Barcilon told the *New York Times*, "It has been a slow and difficult climb that step after step, centimeter after centimeter, fragment after fragment, carried us to a new reading of the expressive intensity and colors we believed had been irretrievably lost."[39]

Colors were brought to life again, blurry figures were made clear, and layers of grime and glue were carefully washed away. Some areas of the painting were impossible to salvage, so light beige paint was added to help cover the blank areas.

Leonardo's **The Last Supper** *is one of the most well-recognized and often copied paintings in the world.*

"We tried to suggest the image, without repainting it, and we tried to lessen the impact of the blanks, and still make clear what is not original,"[40] explained Giuseppe Basile, former director of Italy's Central Restoration Institute.

From Angels to Battles

Not long after finishing *The Last Supper* and around the time he left Milan in 1499, Leonardo began work on *The Virgin and Child with St. Anne*. Commissioned by the monks of Florence's Santissima Annunziata Church for their high altar, *The Virgin and Child* was to show a grouping of the Virgin Mary; her mother, St. Anne; and the infants Jesus and St. John. Leonardo did a number of sketches for the work, as well as a cartoon ready for painting. However, no paint ever touched this initial conception of the work.

Proper Painting of a Battle Scene

In his notebooks, Leonardo penned a long description of how one should properly paint a large battle scene, advice that modern scholars think he planned to employ in his now lost artwork *The Battle of Anghiari*. He said in part:

The conquerors you will make rushing onwards with their hair and other light things flying on the wind, with their brows bent down, and with the opposite limbs thrust forward ... And if you make any one fallen, you must show the place where he has slipped and been dragged along the dust into blood stained mire; and in the half-liquid earth around show the print of the tramping of men and horses who have passed that way. Make also a horse dragging the dead body of his master, and leaving behind him, in the dust and mud, the track where the body was dragged along. You must make the conquered and beaten pale, their brows raised and knit, and the skin above their brows furrowed with pain, the sides of the nose with wrinkles going in an arch from the nostrils to the eyes, and make the nostrils drawn up ... and the lips arched upwards and discovering the upper teeth; and the teeth apart as with crying out and lamentation ... Others represent shouting with their mouths open, and running away. You must scatter arms of all sorts among the feet of the combatants, as broken shields, lances, broken swords and other such objects. And you must make the dead partly or entirely covered with dust, which is changed into crimson mire where it has mingled with the flowing blood.[1]

The horses in this copy of Leonardo's The Battle of Anghiari *by Peter Paul Rubens contain as much personality and individuality as the human figures.*

1. Leonardo Da Vinci, "Of the Way of Representing a Battle," in *The Notebooks of Leonardo da Vinci*. Trans. Jean Paul Richter, Project Gutenberg, 2004. www.gutenberg.org/cache/epub/5000/pg5000.html.

For reasons that are unclear, the artist abandoned it.

The cartoon, today generally called the *Burlington House Cartoon* (after an English art collection that once owned it), is a magnificent work that some art critics and historians prefer over the later painting Leonardo did of the same subject. That later work, which replaced St. John with a lamb and shows Mary, St. Anne, and Jesus in different poses from the ones in the earlier version, was completed sometime between 1507 and 1513. Although some critics do not believe the painting measures up to the original drawing, it is still considered a great painting.

During the long period in which Leonardo worked on the different versions of *The Virgin and Child with St. Anne*, he also devoted time to various stages of other painting projects. One of the biggest was *The Battle of Anghiari*, a commission intended to grace an entire inner wall of Florence's Great Council Hall of the Palazzo Vecchio. (Florentines still celebrated Anghiari, a battle fought in 1440 in which they defeated the forces of their archrival, Milan.) The mural was intended to face a similar painting—*Battle of Cascina* by the great Michelangelo, Leonardo's younger rival—which had been commissioned for the opposite wall.

Unfortunately, Leonardo's painting was never completed, and even the parts the artist did finish did not survive. Not long after he began work, a particularly harsh storm struck Florence, bringing with it extreme humidity that kept the paint from drying. When Leonardo and his assistants tried to force-dry it using a fire, most of the existing paint melted off the wall. In a fit of anger and despair, the artist gave up on the project.

Nevertheless, several of Leonardo's preparatory drawings for the painting have survived, as have drawings and paintings by other artists based on the images on the wall before they were destroyed. These indicate that if *The Battle of Anghiari* had come to fruition, it would have been an artistic masterpiece of epic proportions. Some idea of the awesome concepts Leonardo had in mind for it can be seen in a long passage in his notebooks in which he explained how to paint a battle scene. Leonardo wrote,

You must represent the smoke of artillery mingling in the air with the dust and tossed up by the movement of horses and the combatants ... The higher the smoke mixed with the dust-laden air rises towards a certain level, the more it will look like a dark cloud; and ... will assume a bluish tinge ... If you introduce horses galloping outside the crowd, make the little clouds of

A Controversial Project

In late 2011, researchers found evidence that Leonardo's abandoned painting *The Battle of Anghiari* may still exist on a wall within the Palazzo Vecchio. Leonardo began the work in 1504, but gave up on it about a year later after the experimental new painting technique he was using did not go as planned and a bad storm further ruined his progress. About 50 years later, Giorgio Vasari was hired to renovate the part of the Palazzo Vecchio where Leonardo's unfinished painting was located and instructed to paint his own mural, *The Battle of Marciano in Val di Chiana*.

Leonardo's *Battle of Anghiari* was considered a lost work for more than 500 years, though some art historians suspected that it might still exist. In a controversial move, researchers drilled seven small holes through Vasari's *Battle of Marciano*. They then used tiny probes and high-tech tools to look behind the wall on which Vasari's mural was painted and take samples. What they found shocked the art world. Behind the outer wall was a small air gap and then another wall. On this second wall, researchers "found traces of pigments that appear to be those known to have been used exclusively by Leonardo."[1] Had Vasari been hesitant to paint directly over Leonardo's work? This is what some believe.

Unfortunately, Leonardo's long-lost mural may remain hidden forever. Drilling through Vasari's work was frowned upon by many in the art community, despite the fact that, as Terry Garcia of the U.S. National Geographic Society, which funded the research, pointed out, "all of the holes that were put into the mural were either in areas that had been previously restored or in fissures [cracks], so the original Vasari was not touched."[2] As of November 2017, *The Battle of Anghiari* remains hidden, with researchers unsure of how to proceed with its excavation. It seems that even the potential discovery of this "lost Leonardo" is not enough to warrant the destruction of another artist's work.

1. Quoted in Philip Pullella, "Traces of Lost da Vinci Painting Found Hidden Behind Wall After 500 Years, Researchers Claim," *National Post*, March 12, 2012. nationalpost.com/news/leonardo-da-vinci-battle-of-anghiari.
2. Quoted in Pullella, "Traces of Lost da Vinci."

dust distant from each other in proportion to the strides made by the horses ... The air must be full of arrows in every direction, some shooting upwards, some falling, some flying level.[41]

The identity of the woman in the Mona Lisa *continues to puzzle and fascinate historians and art experts.*

The Immortality of the *Mona Lisa*

At the same time that Leonardo was struggling with his great battle painting, he also began working on a portrait that was destined for true immortality. Entire volumes have been written about this one-of-a-kind artwork—the *Mona Lisa*. Roy McMullen, one of the foremost experts on the work, introduces it simply and definitively as "without doubt the most famous work in the entire forty-thousand-year history of the visual arts."[42]

Art historians agree that Leonardo finished the painting in 1507, after about four years of on-and-off work. However, they still disagree about the identities of both the person who commissioned it and the individual portrayed in it. Theories about the subject of the painting range from various Spanish and Italian noblewomen to a man wearing women's clothes. The theory supported by the largest percentage of scholars is that the person in the painting was Lisa Gherardini. She was the wife of a wealthy Italian silk merchant, who, according to this view, commissioned Leonardo to do the portrait.

If this scenario is correct, the merchant never took possession of the work he had paid for. The *Mona Lisa* remained in Leonardo's possession for the rest of his life, apparently because he had an emotional attachment to it and refused to part with it. As art expert Robert Cumming wrote, "It is likely that the painting began as a portrait of a nobleman's wife but became something much more—the image of Leonardo's idea of perfect beauty."[43]

From critics to art lovers, there is general agreement that, aside from Leonardo's technical mastery, the *Mona Lisa* has a mysterious quality that is both compelling and hard to define. This was well articulated not long after the artist's death by Vasari, who wrote,

In this head, whoever wished to see how closely art could imitate nature, was able to comprehend it with ease ... The eyes had that lustre and watery sheen which are always seen in life, and around them were all those rosy and pearly tints, as well as the lashes, which cannot be represented without the greatest subtlety ... The nose, with its beautiful nostrils, rosy and tender, appeared to be alive. The mouth, with its opening, and with its ends united by the red of the lips to the flesh-tints of the face, seemed, in truth, to be not colours but flesh. In the pit of the throat, if one gazed upon it intently, could be seen the beating of the pulse ... And, indeed, in this work of Leonardo's there was a smile so pleasing, that it was a thing more divine than human to behold.[44]

This conviction that the *Mona Lisa* possesses special qualities that appeal to the heart and emotions has not dimmed over the centuries. The eminent 19th-century English art critic Walter Pater wrote, "She is older than the rocks among which she sits. Like the vampire, she has been dead many times, and learned the secrets of the grave; and has been [a] diver in deep seas [of the human imagination]."[45]

Art experts agree that at least part of this mysterious and strangely alluring quality of the painting stems from the incredibly inventive, cleverly unnatural way that Leonardo used light in it. As Stefan Klein pointed out, it is

remarkable how the light pours over Mona Lisa's *body and plays with her fingers, each of which is finely shaded like a miniature sculpture. The hands project far forward to counterbalance the landscape in the distance, which augments [enhances] the* *painting's sense of depth ... Most importantly, the illumination makes* Mona Lisa *appear both animated and mysterious; the distribution of light and shadow foils any attempt to construe [figure out] her frame of mind. Obviously Leonardo calculated the brightness of each and every square inch of his painting to achieve a particular effect. Nevertheless, no detail seems contrived or calculated; the light that falls on the young woman appears quite natural ...*

But a closer look reveals that something is not quite right. The woman is sitting on a [balcony] ... Therefore the illumination would have to come primarily from the open side of the balcony toward the landscape, so we ought to be seeing Mona Lisa *against the light. But in Leonardo's painting, she is illuminated from the front upper left corner ... Leonardo, however, used the laws of optics to such perfect effect that the illusion is not conspicuous ... We simply accept that the young woman looks more real than reality itself. Leonardo did not paint this picture in accordance with reality; he created a new one — a virtual reality.*[46]

An Accidental Loss

Over the years, a number of people, both experts and average people, have noticed and remarked about the fact that the woman in Leonardo's *Mona Lisa* has no eyebrows. Noted art historian Robert Cumming addressed this point, writing,

> The most likely explanation for [the lady's lack of eyebrows] is that Leonardo did put in eyebrows as a final touch onto the dry paint of the face, but the first time it was cleaned (perhaps in the 17th century), the restorer used the wrong solvent [cleaning fluid] and the eyebrows dissolved and were removed forever. It serves as a warning of how careful restorers must be.[1]

1. Robert Cumming, *Annotated Art*. New York, NY: Dorling Kindersley, 1995, p. 26.

Lost and Found

People today can enjoy looking at many of Leonardo's paintings. However, several have been lost—or presumed lost over the centuries. For example, evidence indicates that in 1506, France's King Louis XII commissioned the artist to create a portrait of Jesus Christ. The work, titled *Salvator Mundi* ("Savior of the World"), was supposedly completed in 1513. Leonardo had it in his possession, but after his death in 1519, it is not clear where the painting went. Although several copies of the work were painted later by his assistants or other well-known artists, the whereabouts of the original remained unknown.

In 2011, however, one of those copies, long assumed to have been created by one of Leonardo's apprentices, was discovered to be the real thing. Its true identity had been hidden because it had been overpainted at least once by an artist whose talent was clearly inferior to Leonardo's. Over five years, art experts removed paint, took high-resolution photos and X-rays, and put the painting under infrared light to authenticate the work as Leonardo's original. Pietro Marani, a Milan-based, world-renowned expert on Leonardo, said, "The blues and the reds in the painting are very similar to those of Da Vinci's Last Supper and the pigment is also very similar to his Virgin of the Rocks painting."[47]

Salvator Mundi shows a calm and relaxed Jesus staring out at the viewer, with his right hand raised as if to give a blessing. His left hand holds a crystalline globe that appears to represent Earth or the entire universe. The painting's powerful portrayal of the human face, rich colors, and technical mastery all combine to form an image no less exquisite and moving than that of the *Mona Lisa*. Both pictures live on to testify

Leonardo's skill at drawing realistic hands is especially evident in Salvator Mundi.

to the artistic genius of the man who created them.

In November 2017, *Salvator Mundi* sold for a record $450 million at a Christie's New York Auction House event. It was the highest price ever paid for a single painting, and far surpassed the $100 million the auction house had predicted it would bring in. Alan Wintermute, Christie's Senior Specialist of Old Master Paintings, told CNN, "The 'Salvator Mundi' is the Holy Grail of Old Master paintings … Long known to have existed, and long sought after, it seemed just a tantalizingly, unobtainable dream until now."[48] Before being identified as an original work by Leonardo in 2011, the painting sold for $60 in a 1958 Christie's auction. Today, *Salvator Mundi* is at the Louvre Museum in Abu Dhabi, which is the capital of the United Arab Emirates. The Saudi prince Bader bin Abdullah bin Mohammed bin Farhan al-Saud bought the painting and then the museum acquired the work.

Ideal Cities and Unfinished Horses

Leonardo was an astounding painter, but that talent alone is not what made him a Renaissance man, universal genius, and polymath. It was his brilliance in multiple areas, including architecture and sculpture. Most of his proposed architectural and sculptural projects never became reality, but his many preliminary drawings and sketches, plus project descriptions surviving in his notes or letters by others, provide valuable information about them. Much of this evidence provides a fairly good idea of what these artworks would have looked like. In addition, for his proposed large-scale sculptures such as revolving cranes, spring motors, and water meters, Leonardo designed a new metal-casting process that strongly influenced all later European sculptors. As Carlo Pedretti, a former Armand Hammer Chair of Leonardo Studies at the University of California, Los Angeles, stated, Leonardo's drawings and futuristic concepts show the world the artist's "insatiable curiosity about the way nature works and the great respect he felt for it."[49]

Dreams of Building

Leonardo's writings clearly reflect his ongoing fascination with architecture and his passion for designing cathedrals. His notes and drawings are alive with renditions of church interiors and exteriors, including large domes atop the roofs. It must have been thrilling for him, therefore, when he heard in 1487 that Milan's government wanted to add a new *tiburio*, or domed tower, on the roof of the city's main cathedral. A competition was held to select the architect for this project and, after conceiving a design, Leonardo hired a carpenter named Bernardo di Abbiate to construct a large, detailed model of his proposed addition.

When presenting his design for the dome, Leonardo included a formal cover letter, which has survived. In it, among other things, he compared the work of an architect to that of a doctor, writing, "You know that medicines, when they are properly used, restore health to invalids, and that he who knows [such medicines] thoroughly ... will be a more effective healer than any other. This too is what the sick cathedral needs—it needs a doctor-architect, who understands the nature of the building, and the laws upon which correct construction is based."[50]

The contest attracted a number of excellent architects, so Leonardo faced stiff competition. In the end, he did not win, but he did not lose either. "The whole affair was quite complicated," Bramly pointed out.

On May 31, [1490], the architects [including Leonardo] met to try to devise a compromise. They discussed it at length without managing to agree ... Finally, all the competitors met for one last discussion ... in front of Lodovico himself ... The final design was [an] amalgam [combination] of all the entries submitted. It is possible that Francesco di Giorgio ... worked out the final design in conversation with Leonardo.[51]

Other architectural projects that Leonardo partially or fully designed but that never actually broke ground include a summer villa for an Italian nobleman, which was designed in 1501. Plans included large, airy rooms, elegant porches, and garden walkways. Some evidence suggests that he also intended to erect a replica of a Roman temple to the goddess Venus and a man-made lake on the villa's grounds.

The Ideal City

In a project that clearly demonstrates the scope of Leonardo's imagination and talents, the artist made plans for what he termed "the ideal city." He was initially inspired to create this city when the plague had raced through Milan, killing almost one-third of the population. He wanted to prevent the spread of a similar disease by building a city that had better communication and sanitation systems. His ideas included a series of canals that would work, in part, as a sewage system, plus upper and lower streets that would separate the classes and hopefully restrict contagious contact. Of course, his city would also include large arches and pillars for aesthetic reasons. While Leonardo's ideas had merit, they would have involved tearing down the city of Milan and starting over—far too large and overwhelming a project for anyone to initiate.

In 1517, Leonardo began designing a new palace complex for the French king. This project never got started, but architectural historians think the plans for it were so impressive that they strongly influenced the next generation of French architects. Some of the royal buildings erected in France in the following centuries likely owed part of their shape and charm to Leonardo's drawings.

In the 1950s, a model of Leonardo's ideal city (shown here) was built to give a greater idea of the shape of his plans.

It would have been fascinating to see how Leonardo's ideal city would have turned out. Shown here are sketches of part of the monumental project.

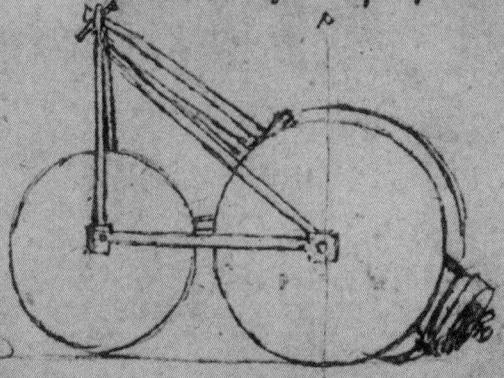

An Inferior Art Form

Leonardo's writings about sculpture made it very clear why he thought it was inferior to painting. In his notebooks, he wrote,

> I myself, having exercised myself no less in sculpture than in painting and doing both one and the other in the same degree, it seems to me that I can ... pronounce an opinion as to which of the two is of the greatest merit and difficulty and perfection ...

> If you will have me only speak of painting on panel [wood], I am content to pronounce between it and sculpture; saying that painting is the more beautiful and the more imaginative and the more copious [plentiful], while sculpture is the more durable but it has nothing else. Sculpture shows with little labor what in painting appears a miraculous thing to do ... In fact, painting is adorned with infinite possibilities which sculpture cannot command.[52]

Despite his obvious disdain for sculpture, Leonardo was not above dabbling in the art form. As in his architectural pursuits, few of the sculptures he designed ever became finished products. However, his sketches and the surviving comments of his contemporaries reveal that he had the potential to become one of the finest sculptors of the Renaissance.

Leonardo crafted his first sculptures during his long apprenticeship to Verrocchio. In his biography of Leonardo, Vasari mentioned that he "worked in sculpture" in his master's studio, "making in his youth, in clay, some heads of women that are smiling, of which plaster casts are still taken, and likewise some heads of boys which appeared to have issued from the hand of a master."[53] Another sculpted piece attributed to Leonardo is a 13-inch (33 cm) tall terra-cotta (baked clay) head generally referred to as *Cristo Fanciullo*, or *Young Christ*. A later owner of the head, Giovanni Paolo Lomazzo, wrote, "I have also a little terracotta head of Christ when he was a boy, sculpted by Leonardo Vinci's own hand, in which one sees the simplicity and purity of the boy, together with a certain something which shows wisdom, intellect, and majesty."[54]

Some art historians have suggested that Leonardo was also the true artist who created the sculpture *The Lady with the Primroses*, long attributed to Verrocchio. According to *Encyclopedia Britannica*, this work "created a new type of Renaissance bust, in which the arms of the sitter are included in the manner of ancient Roman models. This compositional device allows the hands, as well as the face, to express the character and mood of the sitter."[55]

Among the other sculptures that Leonardo may have created while working in Verrocchio's studio are two terra-cotta angels. A number of modern experts think they are Leonardo's because of their close resemblance to the angel he painted in Verrocchio's *Baptism of Christ*. Another similar sculpted angel, also attributed to Leonardo, was found in modern times in a church in northern Italy's hilltop village of San Gennaro. Noted novelist and researcher Charles Nicholl described it as "a beautiful piece, alert and full of movement," adding that "the angel's right arm is an unmistakable echo of the Annunciation angel [attributed to Leonardo], and the long curling hair is a Leonardo trademark."[56] Nicholl thinks Leonardo sculpted the angel in 1477 while passing through the region, perhaps to earn some extra money for his personal expenses. If this is true, the piece has probably been in the little church ever since, long unbeknownst to the art world.

Il Cavallo

For Leonardo, these small, youthful sculptures were completely overshadowed when, in 1483, Duke Ludovico commissioned him to build a gigantic bronze horse statue. The statue was to show the duke's father, Francesco Sforza, atop a magnificent horse. Various modern estimates have been made of the original specifications for the monument. One estimate suggests the finished sculpture would have stood 24 feet (7.3 m) high and weighed 80 tons (72.6 mt). That would have made it more than twice as high and many times as massive as any other horse sculpture that then existed.

Leonardo was eager to create the great statue *Il Cavallo* or "the horse." He told Duke Ludovico, "The bronze horse … is to be the immortal glory and eternal honor of the prince, your father, of happy memory, and of the illustrious house of Sforza."[57] Wanting to do a good job, Leonardo spent a great deal of time preparing for the project, including making many drawings of horses that he studied at nearby stables. Among these drawings are some quick, often disconnected notebook entries recording some of his scattered thoughts about molding such a bulky horse statue. "Make the horse on legs of iron, strong and well set on a good foundation," he began.

Draw upon the horse, when finished, all the pieces of the mould with which you wish to cover the horse, and in laying on the clay cut it in every piece, so that when the mould is finished you can take it off, and then recompose it in its former position …

The clay should be mixed with sand.

Take wax, to return [what is not used] and to pay for what is used.

Dry it in layers.

Make the outside mould of plaster, to save time in drying and the expense in wood ... make terra cotta. And this mould can be made in one day; half a boat load of plaster will serve you.

Good.

Dam it up again with glue and clay, or white of egg, and bricks and rubbish.[58]

Leonardo had more than enough vision and ingenuity to make this statue, but he faced a great obstacle with the casting, as no one had ever attempted to cast such a huge, immensely heavy mass of bronze before. Most Italian artists—including even the great sculptor Michelangelo—considered it impossible. Michelangelo and Leonardo often fought, and one of their confrontations centered on the incomplete statue. The two men supposedly passed each other on the street several years later, and Michelangelo shouted, "You are the one who made a design for a horse to be cast in bronze, and you couldn't cast it!" Turning on his heel, he started to storm away, but then spun around and yelled, "And those Milanese idiots believed in you?"[59]

Although Leonardo did not make the horse sculpture, he did invent a new technique for sectional molding, or piece molding. In this complex process, several molds are made from a clay model, and then liquid bronze is poured into the open space of the molds. By using this method, artists can make initial models of their projects to check for problems or flaws and then correct them before starting the actual statue.

Although Leonardo would not end up casting the horse statue, the large clay model he made of it had made him famous throughout Italy. The people of Milan were proud of the clay giant.

Duke Ludovico worked hard to get enough bronze to make his statue, but by the time he had it, the French were threatening northern Italy. Ludovico then ordered the metal instead be used to make cannons. Leonardo's massive clay model was sitting in a Milan courtyard when the French entered the city in 1499. French archers began using it for target practice. Soon, the weather reduced it to a formless mound of moldy clay. Sadly, the seemingly countless hours Leonardo had put into the project came to nothing.

In 1511, at almost 60 years old, Leonardo came close to getting a second chance to sculpt a huge horse monument. Gian Giacomo Trivulzio, a Milanese military officer in service to the French, asked the aging artist

Although Leonardo and Michelangelo (shown here) had a great deal in common, they were never friends and often argued.

to sculpt a life-size horse and rider for Trivulzio's future tomb. The base of the statue would serve as a marble sarcophagus, or coffin. Leonardo's surviving drawings of the statue show that the horse and rider would have assumed a dramatic, exciting pose. Also, the pedestal on which the horse was to stand would have been beautifully decorated with eight pillars and elaborate carvings. Leonardo's notes about the project even detailed the chemicals needed for the project and what machinery would be needed to cast the figures.

Leonardo made many sketches for the Trivulzio monument. Had the statue been completed, it would most likely have been one of the artist's greatest accomplishments.

A Horse Reborn

In 1966, retired airline pilot and amateur sculptor Charles Dent saw copies of Leonardo's designs for the bronze horse statue. He wanted to see if the horse could finally come to life and be given to the people of Italy in appreciation for all Leonardo had given to the world. Dent knew he could not possibly recreate the master artist's original plans, but he wanted to try to build a monument to the idea. As Dent stated, "It is the gesture itself which is most important."[1]

In 1982, Dent formed Leonardo da Vinci's Horse, Inc., and everyone from sculptors to teachers to horse lovers joined and donated. Thanks to donors across the globe, as well as the money from Dent's will when he passed away in 1994, the bronze horse was finally built. It was installed in Milan's San Siro Hippodrome Cultural Park on September 10, 1999—five centuries from when French archers had used the original model for target practice. While it does not feature the rider shown in the original plans, it is still an incredible testament to one of history's most talented artists and an unrealized dream. Since then, a number of sculptors in the United States and other countries have created horses modeled after Leonardo's ideas.

1. "The Full Story of Leonardo's Horse," Da Vinci Science Center, accessed on April 25, 2018. www.davincisciencecenter.org/about/leonardo-and-the-horse/the-full-story-of-leonardos-horse/.

The Milan horse is 24 feet (7.3 m) tall and weighs 15 tons (13.6 mt).

However, real life once again interfered with the artist's hopes and plans. In 1512, a combined army of Swiss, Spanish, and other forces drove the French, including Trivulzio, out of Milan. Leonardo had lost both his new patron and his last chance for creating a major sculptural legacy. Centuries later, just his sketches for these statues would be considered priceless art treasures and his influence helped future artists create more accurate horse statues.

Faces to Flight: The Drawings

When a retired French doctor decided to have some of the drawings he had inherited from his father valued in 2016, he had no idea what was about to happen. The intentionally anonymous doctor brought in more than a dozen old drawings to the Tajan auction house. One of those drawings was a 530-year-old pen and ink sketch done by Leonardo da Vinci. "My eyes jumped out of their sockets," admitted Carmen C. Bambach, curator of Italian and Spanish drawings at the Metropolitan Museum of Art. "My heart will always pound when I think about that drawing."[60] The 7.5 inch by 5 inch (19 cm by 12.7 cm) sketch is of the Christian martyr St. Sebastian bound to a tree and is estimated to be worth almost $16 million.

Art experts believe that Leonardo drew upward of 2,100 drawings during his lifetime. About 600 of those have survived. He used a number of writing instruments to draw, including black and red chalk, pen and ink, silverpoint (a silver wire or sharpened silver rod), and brushes.

A Range of Human Knowledge

It is challenging to begin to categorize the subjects of Leonardo's drawings as they cover so many types of knowledge. Many of his sketches were simply preliminary studies for his paintings and sculptures, and a number of those have survived.

Conversely, many of Leonardo's drawings were independent studies. Many explored the beauty of the human form, while others captured the complexity of animals, trees, mountains, running water, and other natural forms. Some focused on the intricate workings of architectural and mechanical objects, including the artist's own ingenious inventions. Overall, Wasserman pointed out, these drawings were Leonardo's way of creating "records of visual reality," so that he could better understand "animate and inanimate nature, its form, structure, movement, dynamics, individual character, and force—and where [humans were] concerned, expression."[61]

Regardless of their subject, Leonardo's drawings were almost always extremely detailed and thorough, yet very few of them were ever turned into physical, workable versions. As Wallace explained,

> The meticulousness [exactness] of his drawings indicates ... that he harbored at least the thought of putting his ideas into practice. But he never did. Leonardo always seemed to go on to other things before he took the final step of bringing his projects to concrete, functioning reality. His notes and drawings remained his own secret. He did not allow them to be examined, tested, or put to use.[62]

Leonardo was always more of an artist than a scientist. Art is subjective and can be evaluated and judged privately by anyone, while science must be reviewed and evaluated in the open, in the practical world. The solitary Leonardo dealt with that world only when he had to, and in so doing barred himself from becoming a formal, accomplished scientist.

The Familiar and the Sacred

Among the most striking of Leonardo's surviving drawings are his portraits of men and women of varying ages. Several are studies of the face of the Virgin Mary, a character he painted frequently. He typically depicted her with soft, attractive features and a modest smile. Other portraits are of people Leonardo knew.

There are also a number of self-portraits among Leonardo's drawings. One of these self-portraits, known as the Turin drawing, is particularly famous. It dates from 1512, when Leonardo was 60. Done in red chalk, probably shortly before he departed Milan for Rome, it shows him balding in front and wearing a thick white beard. Bramly wrote,

> Leonardo manages to create a soft image without losing any precision of line or form. Every hair is there ... [By this time] his health was failing, age and long study had weakened his eyes [and] under the light mustache,

This supposed self-portrait shows Leonardo as both gentle and fading.

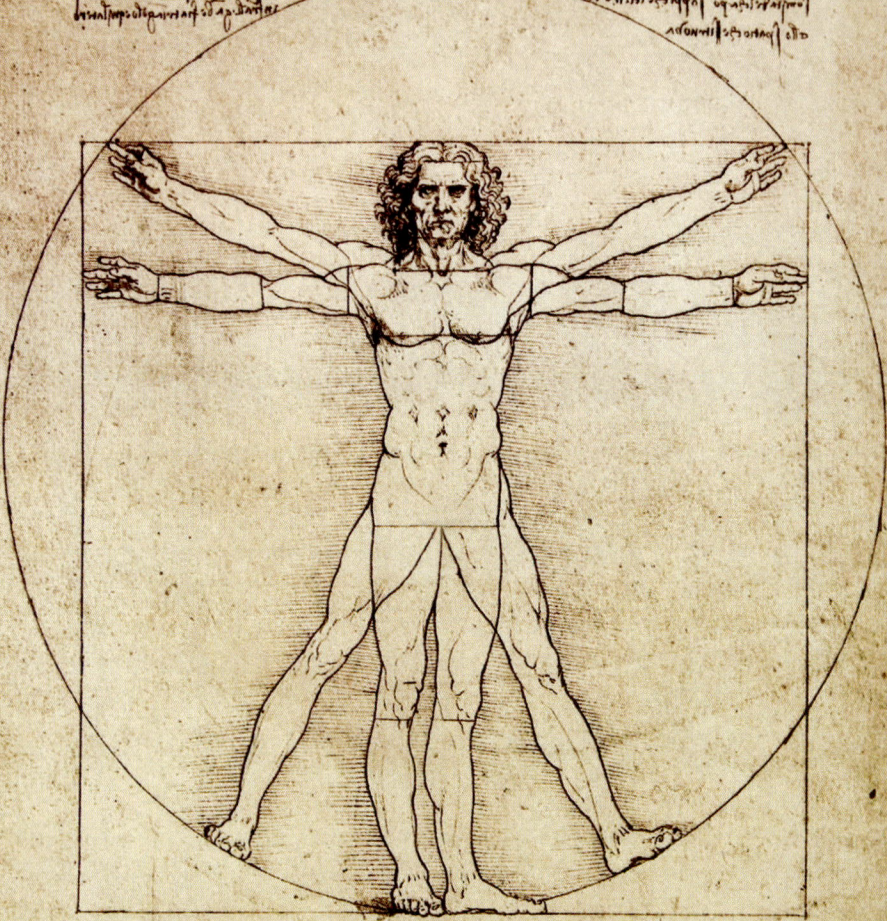

Out of hundreds of surviving drawings by Leonardo, the Vitruvian Man is the one most often associated with the artist. Some art experts theorize that the man in the drawing is Leonardo himself.

the shrunken upper lip reveals that his teeth had gone ... In this portrait, there would be no self-deception. Rather, he was studying himself scientifically, catching himself unawares, so to speak. He scrutinized the worn features of the old man he had become, as if they were those of a stranger. The mysterious power of the drawing may derive from this. Leonardo is summing up his life with a crayon.[63]

The face of the famous *Vitruvian Man*, a Leonardo drawing dating from circa 1490, may be based on that of its creator. This sketch, often used in modern media, shows a naked man's body, with arms outstretched, superimposed on that of another man. Both figures are standing within a large circle. The drawing was intended to show the geometric ratios of the human body. Nicholl wrote, "The stern-looking man in the circle seems to be someone, rather than a cipher," or generic individual. That someone has "penetrating, deeply shadowed eyes, and a thick mane of curly hair." At the least, "there are elements of self-portraiture in the *Vitruvian Man* ... this figure that represents natural harmonies also represents the man uniquely capable of understanding them—the artist-anatomist-architect Leonardo da Vinci."[64]

Exploring the Grotesques

In addition to studies of typical people, Leonardo produced numerous drawings of oddly shaped, exotic-looking individuals, referred to as "grotesques." These people frequently had overly large noses, chins, or other features; few or no teeth; and either menacing demeanors or highly unusual personalities.

The most famous example is a large drawing Leonardo did in the early 1490s. It displays five characters, all positioned close together. The central figure, versions of which appear in many of Leonardo's sketches, has a huge hooked nose and wears a crown of oak leaves, as if pretending to be an emperor. Of the four faces surrounding him, one is in the midst of a wild laugh or scream. The second is seemingly lost in thought; the third displays a demonic grin complete with rotten teeth; and the fourth has a protruding lower lip and puffy jowls. To this date, no one knows what Leonardo was thinking when he sketched these figures.

Leonardo also put enormous amounts of time and energy into reproducing the intricate beauty of the bones, muscles, and organs of the human body. His numerous anatomical drawings were the end result of long hours spent dissecting corpses, primarily at the University of Pavia's medical school, in a town lying about 20 miles (32 km) south of Milan.

Some of the images Leonardo created were not pleasant to look at.

Leonardo intended eventually to collect all of his anatomical drawings and publish them as a major treatise on anatomy. Had he done so, Martin Clayton pointed out, "he would have transformed the study of human anatomy in Europe."[65] Regrettably, however, the aging artist never managed to find the time to complete this task. As a result, his anatomical drawings ended up buried amid piles of writings and sketches, most of which were not made public or thoroughly examined by scholars until modern times.

These truly masterful anatomical drawings present both exterior and interior views of nearly every part of the human body. Moreover, the level of detail and accuracy is often extraordinary, making them examples of both great art and great science. From their comprehensive study of these sketches, scholars Martin Clayton and Ron Philo pointed out one page that includes muscles of the arm, shoulder, hand, and face:

Leonardo fits a remarkable amount of information onto this page ...

These studies of the facial muscles are astonishingly accurate. The drawing to the left [of the page] depicts the superficial [outer] muscles, notoriously difficult to dissect as they may originate and/ or insert into the deep surface of the skin. In the drawing at centre, some of the superficial muscles have been removed to reveal the deeper structures. Though Leonardo did not distinguish formally between the ... muscles of facial expression and the primary muscles of mastication [chewing], he did attempt to identify the function of each. [He also drew] the complex of muscles that raise the upper lip [and] in a note Leonardo reminds himself to see if this is the same muscle that raises the [nostrils] of the horse, an action that he had examined in his studies for the Battle of Anghiari five years earlier.[66]

Weapons of War

In addition to his representations of human faces and bodies, Leonardo turned out numerous drawings of forts, fortifications, and other defensive facilities, as well as weapons of war during his years working for Duke Ludovico and Cesare Borgia. In 1502, Leonardo designed fortifications for Borgia, who had recently taken over Italy's port city of Piombino. Leonardo's sketches indicate four main projects for the town. One was to dig a trench 1,260 feet (384 m) long from the citadel, or main fort, to a nearby peninsula. Defenders would have been able to hide in the trench and direct their fire against invaders landing in boats and trying to attack

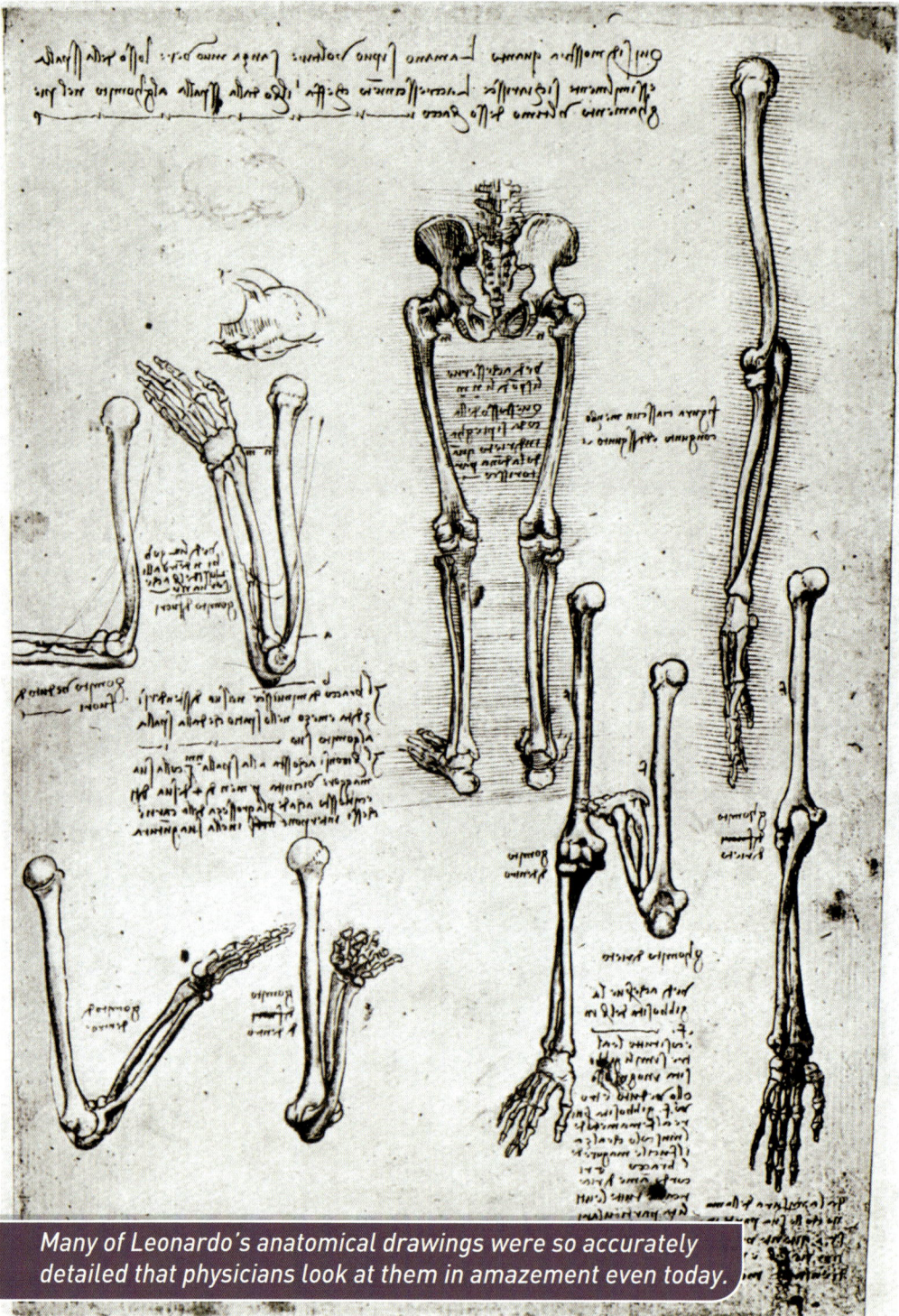

Many of Leonardo's anatomical drawings were so accurately detailed that physicians look at them in amazement even today.

the citadel. The second proposed project was a 590-foot (180 m) long tunnel, running from the citadel to the town gate to provide an escape route, if necessary, for those defending the citadel. Third, Leonardo designed a new, larger tower for the citadel, and fourth, he planned to level a nearby hill so the defenders could achieve a more effective line of fire against an approaching enemy.

Two years earlier, when visiting Venice, Leonardo had designed fortifications and offensive weapons for the local leaders. At the time, Venice was under threat from a Turkish land army and fleet. Leonardo drew a map and on one side sketched his plan to stop the invading land troops by flooding the valley through which they planned to approach the city. (It is unknown whether the Venetians actually built and used any of these devices.) Leonardo even had plans for a submarine; however, he kept his sketches secret. He said that he would not share them "because of the evil nature of men who practice assassination at the bottom of the sea."[67]

Leonardo drew many other offensive weapons. For Duke Ludovico, he designed two lances attached to and protruding from a cavalryman's saddle. These were meant to supplement the rider's handheld lance, as shown in one of Leonardo's sketches. "The tripling of the rider's lance power," scholar Bern Dibner wrote, "must have appealed to Leonardo's penchant [fondness] for designs that multiplied a simple force."[68]

One of the weapons Leonardo drew is a gigantic ballista, or stone thrower, that had been used by the ancient Greeks and Romans. In the sketch, the two large, bow-like arms are constructed in several sections, like a composite bow. Modern experts say this arrangement would have given plenty of flexibility so the ropes attached to their ends could be pulled very far back, creating extra tension. Cradled at the junction of those ropes in the drawing is a huge stone missile. On the sketch's left side, the artist inserted close-ups of two alternate mechanisms for releasing the tension in the ropes and launching the missile. Leonardo also designed a "machine-gun" crossbow based on a team of men walking in a circle to provide rotation for nonstop fire. It was a revolutionary idea for the time.

In a similar vein, Leonardo drew plans for a multiple-barreled light cannon that clearly anticipated the Gatling gun, an early machine-gun invented in the 1800s. He also designed stubby mortars, or short-barreled cannons, that looked exactly like those used in the American Civil War in the 1860s. One scholar asserted that even "a casual examination of some of Leonardo's sketches would indicate that his techniques were those of an artillerist of the mid-1800s. In some respects, he was ahead of even those days."[69]

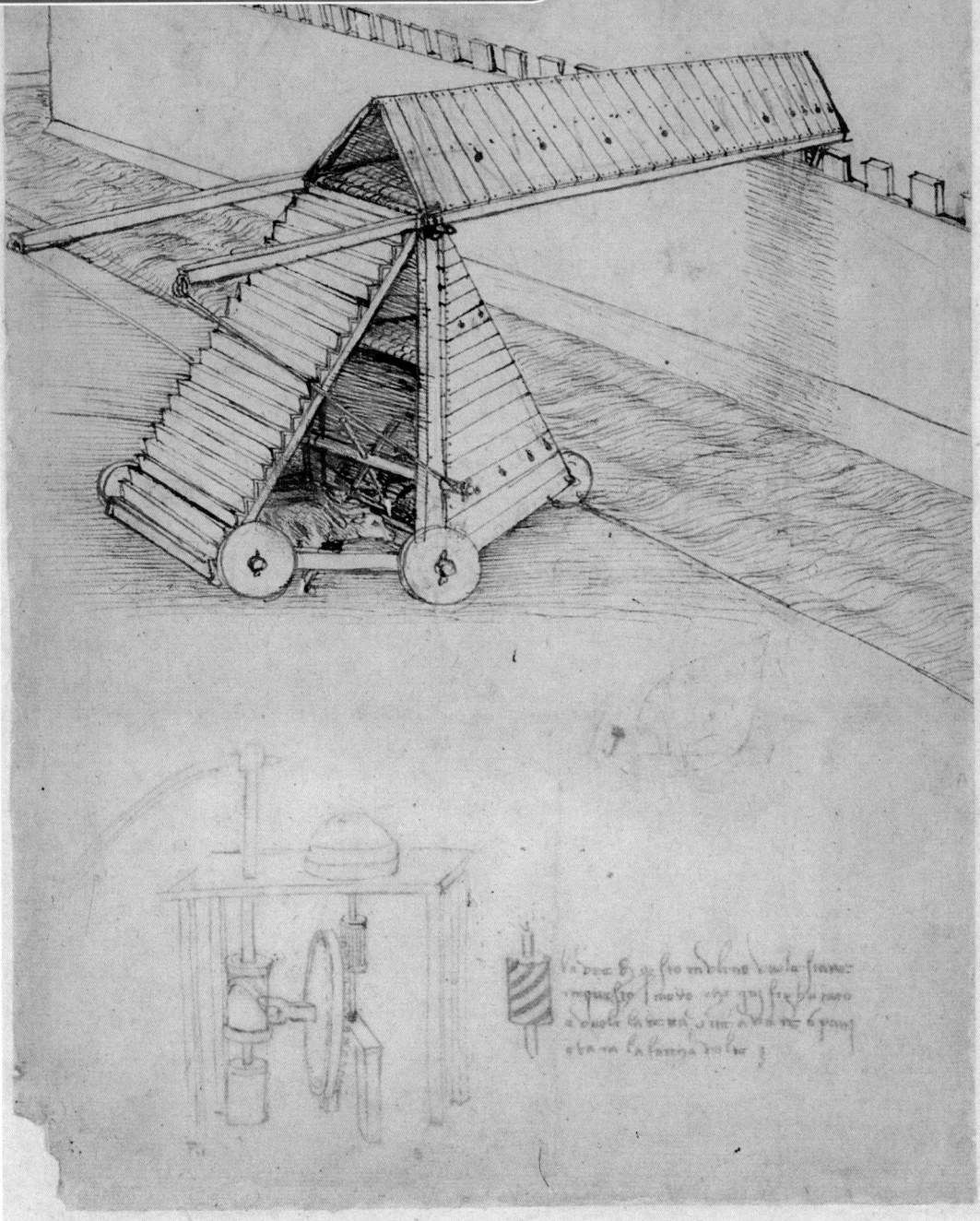

Some of Leonardo's inventions, such as this siege machine designed for crossing walls into an enemy's fortress, would have been quite frightening if put on a battlefield.

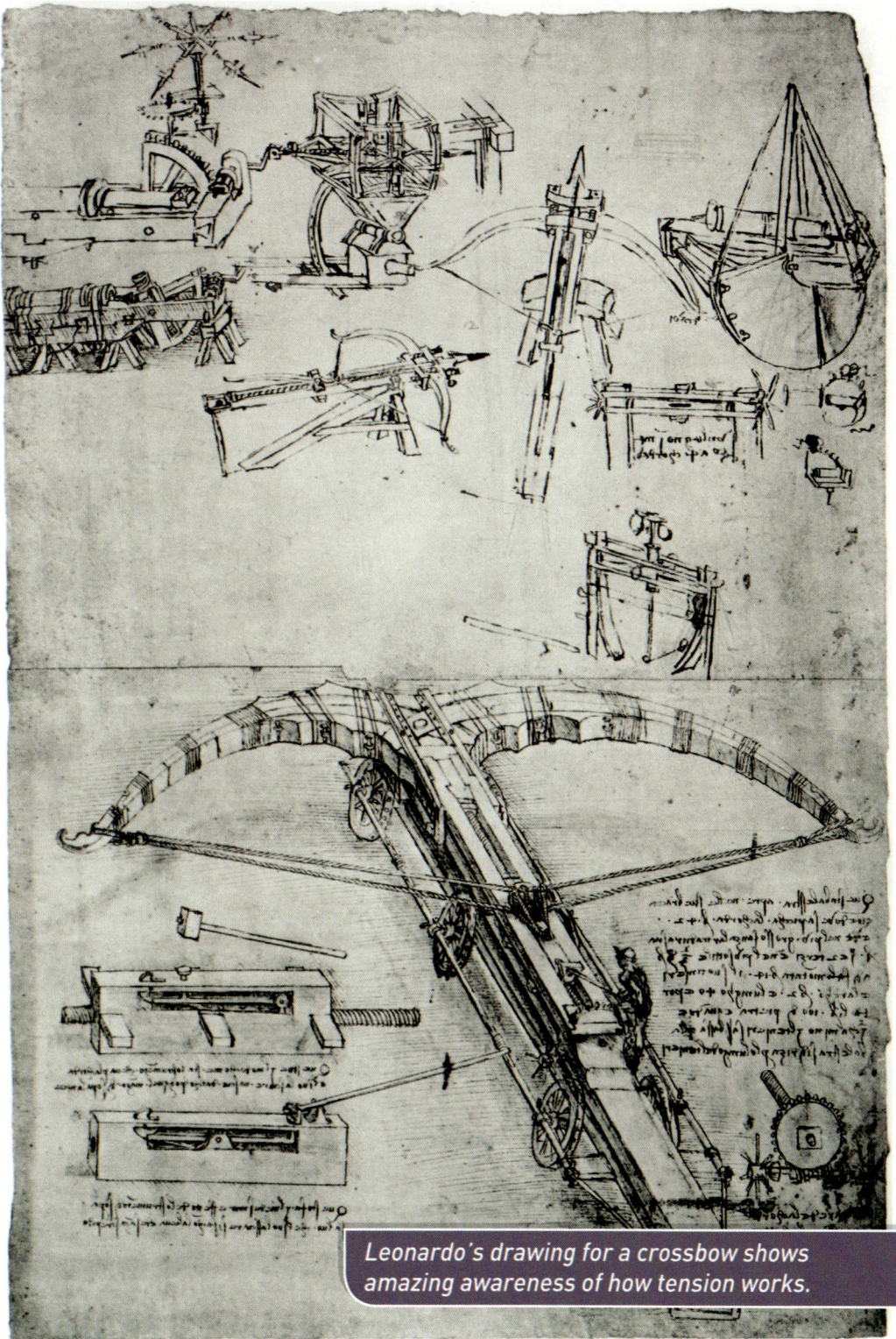

Leonardo's drawing for a crossbow shows amazing awareness of how tension works.

Ahead of His Time

Some of Leonardo's drawings show that he was definitely ahead of his time in his attempts to design a practical way for humans to fly like birds. Among his most famous sketches are studies of birds in flight and of people donning elaborate mechanical wings of his own design. For 25 years, Leonardo studied human flight. Unfortunately, he was approaching the problem from the wrong angle. He long assumed that the only answer was to literally mimic birds—by the flapping of wings. Initially, he did not conceive that a human's arms simply cannot produce enough power to make this possible.

Eventually, Leonardo caught on to the potential of using gliders for human flight. According to Klein,

Leonardo started to realize, during his final years in Milan, that beating wings were insufficient for flight. Humans were simply too weak to rise into the sky on their own power …

He returned to studying nature [and] noticed that the larger the bird, the less frequently it flapped its wings. Now he saw a solution that made it possible to remain aloft for hours …

Leonardo had understood that in gliding the critical element is achieving the optimal shape of the wing. Only then can the wings transform the headwinds into lift.[70]

For reasons that remain uncertain, Leonardo did not follow up on his ideas for gliders. Despite some tales that circulated after his death, as far as modern scholars can tell, he did not actually build a full-sized glider and either pilot it himself or have someone else do so. Some of his other drawings show diverse flight-related inventions, including the parachute, the helicopter, and a device to measure wind speed. That he took the time to draw these things in detail is often seen as an indication that he believed humans would one day fly.

One thing always remained true of Leonardo: He was a man of unending curiosity, which was clearly reflected in his complex drawings. As Leonardo biographer Walter Issacson stated, "Being curious about everything and curious just for curiosity's sake, not simply because it's useful, is the defining trait of Leonardo. It's how he pushed himself and taught himself how to be a genius."[71]

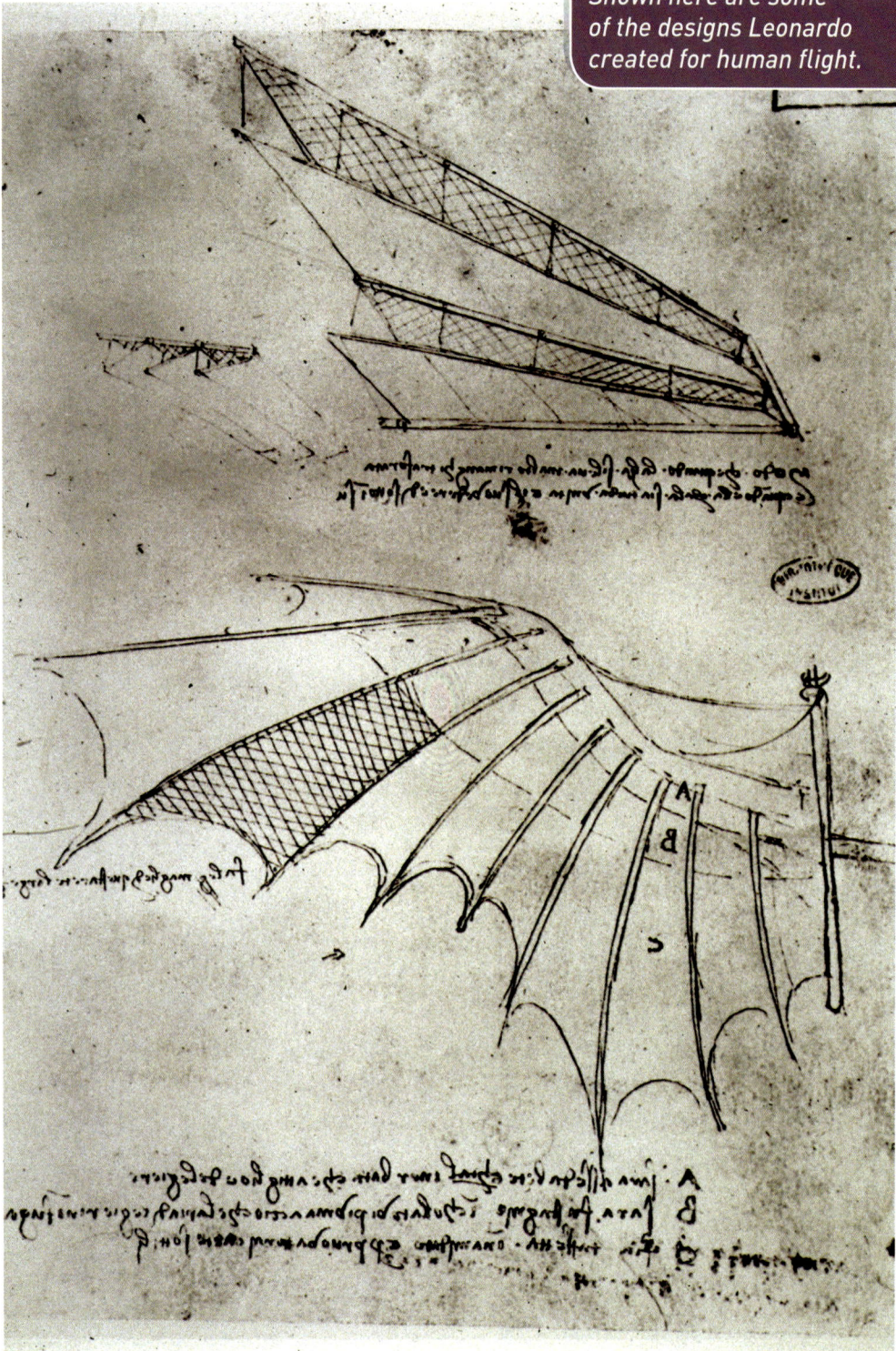

CHAPTER SIX

A Lasting Legend

Leonardo's greatest legacy is that he inspired other artists, inventors, architects, and engineers to keep their ideas evolving and developing. Many of the amazing inventions he developed centuries ago are still used today, in one way or another. Leonardo designed simple items that today people may take for granted such as an effective pair of scissors and a working parachute. He also designed much more complex machines including a human-powered helicopter and a humanoid robot with the ability to raise its arms and move its joints.

As a painter, Leonardo's influence has been extraordinarily far reaching. By early modern times, he had become a household name throughout the Western world, in part because he had created the most famous and beloved painting in history, the *Mona Lisa*. Many artists, art critics, and art historians in the generations that succeeded Leonardo felt the impact of his entire collection of paintings, the *Mona Lisa* in particular.

Many younger painters, including the great Italian Renaissance painter Raphael, held Leonardo and his paintings in awe and closely studied them. When Raphael arrived in Florence in 1504 at the age of 21, he immediately fell under Leonardo's spell. To develop his abilities at portraiture, Raphael created several drawings based on the *Mona Lisa*. "A good example," McMullen wrote,

Leonardo sketched his first ideas for a parachute in the early 1480s.

"is a drawing that has been dated as early as 1504."[72] McMullen added that the details of this drawing's composition were beyond a doubt copied right from the *Mona Lisa*. Like Raphael, numerous later painters studied, copied, and learned from the *Mona Lisa*, *The Last Supper*, *The Virgin of the Rocks*, and other paintings by Leonardo containing human portraits.

A Vision of the Future

Leonardo's artistic legacy contains much more than his influence as a painter, however. Many of his drawings were rooted in the world of his own time, but large numbers of them also depicted ideas and devices that belong to a world that did not yet exist but he hoped to help shape. As Klein wrote,

His sketches offered a vision of a distant future in which people would understand the forces of nature and work with machines. [Of his collected drawings], turning a single page would transport [the viewer] to a very different, though no less fantastic, world. Leonardo used chalk and pen to draw the inside of a human heart and a fetus growing in a womb. Other drawings showed aerial views of Italian landscapes and cities—the way we might see them from an airplane today ...

[Because of such futuristic art] Leonardo is now finally taken seriously not just as [a painter], but also as an explorer of our world ... [In] the past, scholars who studied Leonardo were primarily art historians, [but] when heart surgeons, physicists, and engineers now look at these same projects ... they are amazed at what they find.[73]

Indeed, even before the 20th century, during which science took grand leaps forward, Leonardo's anatomical studies had a profound influence on doctors and the science of medicine. In 1773, noted English anatomist William Hunter visited the library of King George III, where many of Leonardo's old drawings were then stored. There, Hunter became the first trained scientist to examine the sketches in detail since the artist's death more than 250 years before. In a later lecture about Leonardo, Hunter spoke of the artist's influence: "a genius of the first rate, Leonardo da Vinci, who has been overlooked, because he was of another profession, and because he published nothing upon the subject. I believe he was, by far, the best Anatomist ... of his time ... and Leonardo was certainly the first man we know of who introduced the practice of making anatomical drawings."[74]

In a similar manner, Leonardo's far-ranging artistic renderings of

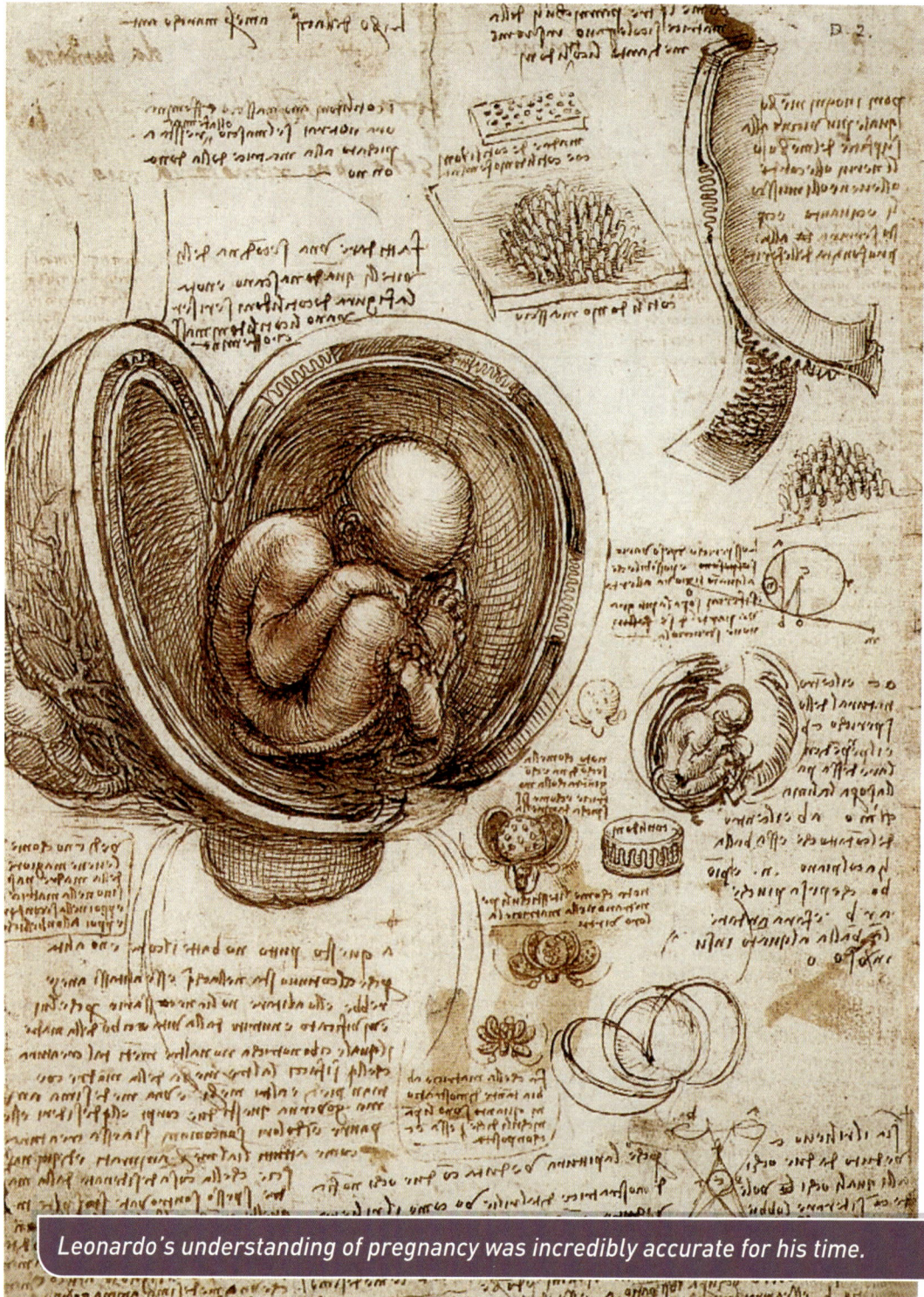

Leonardo's understanding of pregnancy was incredibly accurate for his time.

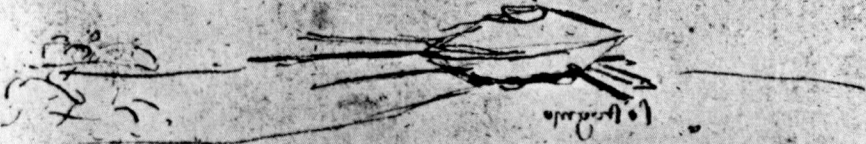

futuristic gadgets had direct influences on a number of key early modern inventors such as Igor Sikorsky. Sikorsky was a Russian American aviation pioneer who built some of the first modern helicopters. According to the National Aviation Hall of Fame,

> One of Sikorsky's earliest recollections is of his mother telling him of Leonardo da Vinci's attempts to design a flying machine. From that moment on the dream of flight captured his imagination, even though he was repeatedly told that flying had been proven impossible. Finally, at the age of about 12, Sikorsky made a model of a crude helicopter. Powered by rubber bands, the model rose into the air. Now he knew that his dream was not a foolhardy impossibility.[75]

A Different Way of Thinking

Leonardo was able to excel in so many areas of human knowledge because his mind had a different way of assimilating and analyzing information than others. As Klein explained, Leonardo

> regarded the world as a single entity and sought similarities between the most dissimilar phenomena. We try to solve problems as systematically [precisely and carefully] as possible; he did so by employing creative combinations. We want answers; he posed questions. But there is nothing to stop us from learning from Leonardo's approach—not to replace the modern way of thinking, but to supplement it. Above all, however, Leonardo demonstrated how far a person can take research that has no set goal. Driven by curiosity, he worked for the sheer pleasure of understanding the world.[76]

Keeping Secrets?

Over the last few decades, a great deal of attention has been given to whether Leonardo was a secretive, even shadowy individual. One factor pointed out was his frequent habit of writing his notes backward, as if trying to hide their content. His failure to publish his writings has also been interpreted by some as an attempt to keep secrets. In addition, there is the mysterious smile on the face of the unidentified woman in the *Mona Lisa*. That unique, puzzling grin has given many people the impression that the artist purposely kept her anonymous.

Experts who have studied Leonardo's life say that none of these factors mean the artist was intentionally secretive. He wrote in mirror images because he was left-handed. He did not publish his writings because he was too busy to do so. Finally, the identity of the model for the *Mona Lisa* was almost certainly known to his circle of acquaintances, and only time has clouded that information.

Nevertheless, Leonardo's reputation as a mystery man persists because it is so well imbedded in the popular consciousness that it is hard to banish with actual evidence. As a result, all sorts of unfounded theories about him have been spread over time, especially in the 20th century.

The most famous example is the ongoing controversy surrounding Leonardo's supposed involvement in a secret society called the Priory of Sion. The discussion began in the 1970s with a low-level French government employee named Pierre Plantard. In various interviews, as well as a 1979 BBC documentary, Plantard claimed that he was both a descendant of medieval French kings and a member of the Priory of Sion. That organization, he said, had existed in secret for many centuries. Its goal was to safeguard the bloodline, or descendants, of Jesus of Nazareth and Mary Magdalene, a woman who traveled with Jesus and his disciples. Jesus and Mary had married and produced children, Plantard theorized, and that bloodline later produced some of the French royals and eventually Plantard himself. Moreover, Plantard claimed, the Priory of Sion had had many formidable leaders over the centuries known as Grand Masters. Supposedly, Leonardo was one of them.

The next link in the chain connecting Leonardo to the secret Priory of Sion was the 1982 nonfiction book *Holy Blood, Holy Grail* by Richard Leigh and Henry Lincoln. The authors elaborated on the story Plantard had told while giving the impression that it might well be true. Later, in 2003, popular novelist Dan Brown published *The Da Vinci Code*. This runaway best seller and its follow-up movie wove an exciting fictional murder-mystery around the "facts" asserted earlier by Plantard, Leigh, and Lincoln. In Brown's book, a man investigating the Priory of Sion finds that Leonardo had left behind clues to the secret about Jesus and Mary Magdalene, including letters and symbols imbedded in code in *The Last Supper* and other paintings.

Needless to say, Brown's book displeased the Catholic Church, which in his story, had long been trying to cover up the "truth" about Jesus and his descendants in order to keep the secret. Critics inside and outside the church have apparently been justified in saying that there is nothing to the story about Jesus's marriage, a secret society, or Leonardo's involvement. Reliable independent scholars report that Plantard almost certainly made up all of it. Most of these experts do not fault Brown, since

The Earliest Robot

Leonardo's marvelous ability to imagine futuristic ideas and machines is no better illustrated than in his designs and working model for an early robot. The robot was centuries ahead of its time:

> Leonardo created his robot to prove to himself that a human being's body could be imitated. He also built it to showcase it in working mode at parties for his patron Lodovico Sforza. The [robot] would have been the highlight of the party with Leonardo at the helm of the crank powering [it] ... Leonardo used his initial studies of anatomy ... to design the robot. His creation was an extension of his hypothesis that the human body is a machine in structure [and] that its intricate movements could be imitated with the use of engineered machine parts such as levers and pulleys. When Leonardo built his Robot in 1495, it had the capability to walk, stand and sit, open and close its mouth, and raise its arms ... [According to Leonardo's drawings] the robot was composed of two working structures. Firstly, there was a four-factor system that controlled the hands, wrists, elbows and shoulders. Secondly, there was a tri-factor system, which controlled the hips, knees and ankles ... The lower body ... was powered by a crank via a cable, which in turn was connected to all the component parts of the leg.[1]

1. "Leonardo da Vinci and His Robots," Leonardo da Vinci Biography. www.leonardo-da-vinci-biography.com/da-vinci-robotic.html.

he only took some existing controversial ideas and used them to craft a suspenseful fictional account. As noted biblical scholar Bart Ehrman said, "I'd say to readers that they should enjoy it as a work of fiction and not take its fictional claims as factual claims."[77]

Leonardo's Genius on Display

Thus, Leonardo emerged from this controversy the same way he entered it—as a brilliant artist whose mind roamed throughout the massive body of human knowledge. His desire to go beyond the limits of painting, sculpture, and other specific disciplines and use his artistic talents to investigate other areas of knowledge made him unique among his peers. As biographer Walter Isaacson said,

> *Thinking for himself, Leonardo questions all received wisdom and says, "Let me test that." It's the beginning of the scientific method. He is the greatest forerunner of that method, in that he kept devising experiments to test*

his theories. And he was willing to revise his theories in light of new facts—it's what made Leonardo great. That and this desire to try to learn everything, a desire that spurs him to be an innovator in so many fields.[78]

To honor Leonardo and his incredible mind, a rotating exhibition of the artist's works began in 2019 in venues across the United Kingdom. The exhibition, titled *Leonardo da Vinci: A Life in Drawings*, features 200 pieces of Leonardo's works that were held in the Royal Collection Trust. In May 2019, in time for the 500th anniversary of Leonardo's death, the drawings will be collected and displayed in an exhibit at the Queen's Gallery in Buckingham Palace.

In a press release for the event, the Royal Collection Trust commented on the depth of Leonardo's knowledge and influence despite so few surviving works:

Revered in his day as a painter, Leonardo completed only around 20 paintings; he was respected as a sculptor and architect, but no sculpture or buildings by him survive; he was a military and civil engineer who plotted with Machiavelli to divert the river Arno, but the scheme was never executed; he was an anatomist and dissected 30 human corpses, but his ground-breaking anatomical work was never published; he planned treatises on painting, water, mechanics, the growth of plants and many other subjects, but none was ever finished. As so much of his life's work was unrealised or destroyed, Leonardo's greatest achievements survive only in his drawings and manuscripts.[79]

The 2019 exhibition at Buckingham Palace is the largest display of works by Leonardo in more than 65 years. The drawings, which were placed in an album by Italian sculptor Pompeo Leoni, have been kept together since 1590. Among them are two seemingly blank pages, which upon exposure to ultraviolet light reveal faded sketches that Leonardo made while preparing to paint *The Adoration of the Magi*. Art historians had discovered that the metallic copper in the stylus Leonardo had sketched with underwent a chemical change over time that caused the drawings to become invisible to the naked eye. With discoveries being made of Leonardo's works even in 2016, it will be exciting to see what long-lost works are uncovered in the future.

Notes

Introduction: A True Polymath

1. Quoted in Omar Ismail, "Leonardo da Vinci on What It Means to Be a Good Painter and How to Become One," Medium, October 28, 2014. medium.com/@omarismail_io/leonardo-da-vinci-on-what-it-means-to-be-a-good-painter-and-how-to-become-one-880bc92a06bd.

2. Leonardo da Vinci, *The Literary Works of Leonardo da Vinci*. Trans. Jean Paul Richter, London, UK: Sampson Low, Marston, Searle & Rivington, 1883, p. 251.

3. Quoted in Robert Payne, *Leonardo*. Garden City, NY: Doubleday, 1978, p. xvii.

4. Giorgio Vasari, "Life of Leonardo da Vinci," trans. Gaston DeC. De Vere. Quoted in *Medieval Sourcebook: Giorgio Vasari: Life of Leonardo da Vinci 1550*. Fordham University, accessed on April 18, 2018. www.fordham.edu/halsall/source/vasari1.html.

5. Serge Bramly, *Leonardo: Discovering the Life of Leonardo da Vinci*. Trans. Sian Reynolds. New York, NY: HarperCollins, 1991, p. 13.

6. Roy McMullen, *Mona Lisa: The Picture and the Myth*. Boston, MA: Houghton Mifflin, 1975, pp. 1–2.

7. Stefan Klein, *Leonardo's Legacy: How Da Vinci Reimagined the World*. New York, NY: Da Capo, 2011, p. 5.

8. Da Vinci, *Literary Works*, p. 463.

Chapter One: A Man Like No Other

9. Quoted in CBS News, "Excerpt: Walter Isaacson's 'Leonardo da Vinci,'" CBS News, October 12, 2017. www.cbsnews.com/news/excerpt-walter-isaacsons-leonardo-da-vinci/.

10. Vasari, "Life of Leonardo da Vinci." Quoted in *Medieval Sourcebook: Giorgio Vasari: Life of Leonardo da Vinci 1550*.

11. Robert Wallace, *The World of Leonardo: 1452–1519*. New York, NY: Time-Life Books, 1981, pp. 13–15.

12. Quoted in da Vinci, *Literary Works*, pp. 326–327.

13. Martin Clayton and Ron Philo, *Leonardo da Vinci: The Mechanics of Man*. Los Angeles, CA: J. Paul Getty Museum, 2010, p. 9.

14. Leonardo Da Vinci, "Of Judging Your Own Pictures," in *The Notebooks of Leonardo da Vinci*. Trans. Jean Paul Richter, Project Gutenberg, 2004. www.gutenberg.org/cache/epub/5000/pg5000.html.

15. Emanuel Winternitz, "Strange Musical Instruments in the Madrid Notebooks of Leonardo da Vinci," *Metropolitan Museum Journal*, 1969, p. 125.

16. Quoted in Payne, *Leonardo*, pp. 182–183.

17. Quoted in Sherwin B. Nuland, *Leonardo da Vinci*. New York, NY: Viking, 2005, pp. 165–166.

18. Quoted in Leonardo da Vinci, *Leonardo da Vinci: Life and Work, Paintings and Drawings*. Ed. Ludwig Goldscheider, New York, NY: Phaidon, 1959, p. 39.

19. Rossella Lorenzi, "Did a Stroke Kill Leonardo da Vinci?," Seeker, May 10, 2016. www.seeker.com/did-a-stroke-kill-leonardo-da-vinci-1789047208.html.

20. Quoted in da Vinci, *Leonardo da Vinci*, p. 39.

Chapter Two: The Beginning Artist

21. Bramly, *Leonardo*, p. 187.

22. Elke Linda Buchholz et al., *Art: A World History*. New York, NY: Abrams, 2007, pp. 144–146.

23. "Baptism of Christ," BBC, accessed on April 30, 2018. www.bbc.co.uk/science/

leonardo/gallery/baptism.
shtml.

24. Jack Wasserman, *Leonardo da Vinci*. New York, NY: Harry N. Abrams, 2003, p. 48.

25. Wasserman, *Leonardo da Vinci*, p. 70.

26. Payne, *Leonardo*, pp. 41–42.

27. Quoted in da Vinci, *Leonardo da Vinci*, p. 15.

28. Da Vinci, *Literary Works*, p. 319.

29. Da Vinci, *Literary Works*, p. 320.

30. Wallace, *World of Leonardo*, p. 35.

31. Wallace, *World of Leonardo*, p. 35.

32. Da Vinci, *Literary Works*, p. 395.

33. Quoted in Jonathan Crow, "Leonardo da Vinci's To Do List (Circa 1490) Is Much Cooler than Yours," Open Culture, December 2, 2014. www.openculture.com/2014/12/leonardo-da-vincis-to-do-list-circa-1490-is-much-cooler-than-yours.html.

34. Quoted in Crow, "Leonardo da Vinci's To Do List."

Chapter Three: New Techniques, New Masterpieces

35. Buchholz et al., *Art*, p. 148.

36. Quoted in Wasserman, *Leonardo da Vinci*, p. 92.

37. Vasari, "Life of Leonardo da Vinci," Quoted in *Medieval Sourcebook: Giorgio Vasari: Life of Leonardo da Vinci 1550.*

38. "The Last Supper," BBC, accessed on April 30, 2018. www.bbc.co.uk/science/leonardo/gallery/lastsupper.shtml.

39. Alessandra Stanley, "After a 20-Year Cleanup, a Brighter, Clearer 'Last Supper' Emerges," *New York Times*, May 27, 1999. www.nytimes.com/1999/05/27/arts/after-a-20-year-cleanup-a-brighter-clearer-last-supper-emerges.html.

40. Stanley, "20-Year Cleanup."

41. Leonardo Da Vinci, "Of the Way of Representing a Battle," in *The Notebooks of Leonardo da Vinci*. Trans. Jean Paul Richter, Project Gutenberg, 2004. www.gutenberg.org/cache/epub/5000/pg5000.html.

42. McMullen, *Mona Lisa*, p. 1.

43. Robert Cumming, *Annotated Art*. New York, NY: Dorling Kindersley, 1995, p. 27.

44. Vasari, "Life of Leonardo da Vinci," Quoted in *Medieval Sourcebook: Giorgio Vasari: Life of Leonardo da Vinci 1550*.

45. Quoted in Klein, *Leonardo's Legacy*, p. 14.

46. Klein, *Leonardo's Legacy*, pp. 29, 32.

47. Quoted in Nick Pisa, "The Painting Once Sold for £45 'Is a Long-Lost Leonardo Worth £120 Million'," DailyMail.com, July 4, 2011. www.dailymail.co.uk/news/article-2010309/Leonardo-Da-Vinci-Is-long-lost-120m-Salvator-Mundi-painting-authentic.html.

48. Charlotte Parsons, "Rediscovered Leonardo da Vinci Painting Expected to Fetch $100M," CNN, November 15, 2017. www.cnn.com/style/article/da-vinci-painting-auction/index.html.

Chapter Four: Ideal Cities and Unfinished Horses

49. George Bushnell, "Leonardo da Vinci as Engineer and Architect […]," *Christian Science Monitor*, July 28, 1987. www.csmonitor.com/1987/0728/lvinci.html.

50. Quoted in Charles Nicholl, *Leonardo da Vinci: Flights of the Mind*. New York, NY: Viking, 2004, p. 223.

51. Bramly, *Leonardo*, p. 211.

52. Da Vinci, *Literary Works*, pp. 329–330.

53. Vasari, "Life of Leonardo da Vinci," Quoted in *Medieval Sourcebook: Giorgio Vasari: Life of Leonardo da Vinci 1550*.

54. Quoted in Rachel Koestler-Grack, *Leonardo da Vinci: Artist, Inventor, and Renaissance Man*. Philadelphia, PA: Chelsea House Publishers, 2006, p. 29.

55. Günter Passavant, "Andrea del Verrocchio," *Encyclopedia Britannica*, last updated May 19, 2017. www.britannica.com/biography/Andrea-del-Verrocchio#ref140539.

56. Nicholl, *Leonardo da Vinci*, p. 125.

57. Da Vinci, *Leonardo da Vinci*, p. 33.

58. Da Vinci, *Notebooks of Leonardo da Vinci*.

59. Quoted in Payne, *Leonardo*, p. 14.

Chapter Five:
Faces to Flight:
The Drawings

60. Anne Quito, "A $16 Million Drawing by Leonardo da Vinci Has Been Found in France," Quartz, December 13, 2016. qz.com/861797/ discovered-a-16-million-leonardo-da-vinci-drawing-of-st-sebastian-was-found-in-france/.
61. Wasserman, *Leonardo da Vinci*, p. 28.
62. Wallace, *World of Leonardo*, p. 110.
63. Bramly, *Leonardo*, pp. 19–20.
64. Nicholl, *Leonardo da Vinci*, p. 147.
65. Clayton and Philo, *Leonardo da Vinci*, p. 8.
66. Clayton and Philo, *Leonardo da Vinci*, p. 124.
67. Quoted in Michele Lent Hirsch, "Step Inside a Famous Submarine," *Smithsonian*, May 26, 2015. www.smithsonianmag.com/ travel/Step-inside-a-famous-submarine-180955042/.
68. Quoted in Ladislao Reti, *The Unknown Leonardo*. New York, NY: Abradale Press, 1990, p. 168.
69. Quoted in Reti, *The Unknown Leonardo*, p. 178.
70. Klein, *Leonardo's Legacy*, p. 116.
71. Quoted in Simon Worrall, "What Made Leonardo da Vinci a Genius?," *National Geographic*, November 4, 2017. news. nationalgeographic. com/2017/11/leonardo-da-vinci-genius-walter-isaacson/.

Chapter Six:
A Lasting Legend

72. McMullen, *Mona Lisa*, p. 28.
73. Klein, *Leonardo's Legacy*, pp. 3, 7.
74. Quoted in Clayton and Philo, *Leonardo da Vinci*, p. 28.
75. "Sikorsky, Igor Ivanovich," National Aviation Hall of Fame, accessed on April 18, 2018. www.nationalaviation. org/sikorsky-igor.
76. Klein, *Leonardo's Legacy*, p. 222.
77. Quoted in Stone Phillips, "Secrets Behind 'The Da Vinci Code,'" Dateline NBC, May 26, 2006. www. msnbc.msn.com/id/7491383/ ns/dateline_nbc/t/secrets-behind-da-vinci-code.

78. Quoted in John Timpane, "Leonardo da Vinci Was a Total Misfit, and His Biographer Says That's Part of His Genius," *Inquirer (Philadelphia)*, November 28, 2017. www.philly.com/philly/entertainment/arts/leonardo-da-vinci-biography-walter-isaacson-20171128.html.

79. "Press Release: Nationwide Exhibitions of Drawings by Leonardo da Vinci from the Royal Collection to Open in 2019," Royal Collection Trust, February 7, 2018. www.royalcollection.org.uk/about/press-office/press-releases/nationwide-exhibitions-of-drawings-by-leonardo-da-vinci-from-the#/.

For More Information

Books

Da Vinci, Leonardo. *The Notebooks of Leonardo da Vinci*. Ed. Edward MacCurdy. London, UK: Arcturus, 2017.
> McCurdy's carefully edited collection of Leonardo's notebooks provides a glimpse into the mind of the master artist.

Isaacson, Walter. *Leonardo da Vinci*. New York, NY: Simon & Schuster, 2017.
> Isaacson's biography of Leonardo is based on the artist's own notebooks.

Phillips, Cynthia, and Shana Priwer. *101 Things You Didn't Know about Da Vinci: Inventions, Intrigue, and Unfinished Works*. Avon, MA: Adams Media, 2018.
> This book is filled with more than 100 amazing facts about the life and work of Leonardo.

Zöllner, Frank. *Leonardo da Vinci, 1452–1519: The Complete Paintings and Drawings*. Köln, Germany: Taschen, 2016.
> This book features all of Leonardo's known works, including nearly 700 of his drawings.

Websites

Da Vinci—The Genius
www.mos.org/leonardo/
> The Boston Museum of Science explores Leonardo's many roles as a Renaissance man, including artist, inventor, and scientist.

Leonardo da Vinci
www.history.com/topics/leonardo-da-vinci
> This History Channel website has videos and an informative biography about Leonardo.

Leonardo da Vinci (1452–1519)
www.metmuseum.org/toah/hd/leon/hd_leon.htm
> The official website of the Metropolitan Museum of Art in New York City has information about Leonardo's life and his works of art.

***Mona Lisa* ... Leonardo's Masterful Technique**
www.pbs.org/treasuresoftheworld/a_nav/mona_nav/mnav_level_1/3technique_monafrm.html
> This PBS website has a wealth of information about Leonardo's *Mona Lisa* and his masterful style of painting.

Index

Picture Credits

About the Author

Tamra B. Orr is the author of more than 500 nonfiction books for readers of all ages. She lives in the Pacific Northwest with her family and spends her free time writing letters to people all over the world and tent camping throughout the state. Orr graduated from Ball State University with a degree in secondary education but found she would rather write about the world than anything else. She has been a longtime admirer of Leonardo da Vinci and hopes that by writing about him, a little of his genius will rub off on her.